NARRATIVE POEMS

C. S. LEWIS

NARRATIVE POEMS

Edited by

WALTER HOOPER

HARCOURT BRACE JOVANOVICH, INC.

New York

CONTENTS

PREFACE

This book contains all the narrative poems by C. S. Lewis which, as far as I know, are extant, and they can be enjoyed without reading the preface, which is not a critical assessment, but is rather intended to provide them with some historical background.

Lewis wrote his first poems in the 'little end room' at his home, Little Lea, in Belfast before he went to his first school at the age of ten. He disliked all the schools he attended and the English ones were given fictitious names in his autobiography, *Surprised by Joy* (1955). Like so many of his prose works, it was originally composed in verse.

The romantic imagination was already strong in Lewis when he went to Wynyard School in Watford, Hertfordshire ('Belsen' in *Surprised by Joy*), where he was a boarder from 1908–10. From Wynyard he was sent to Campbell College, Belfast, for one year (1910) and from there to Cherbourg House in Malvern (called 'Chartres' in his autobiography) where he was a student from 1911–13. It was at Cherbourg House, between the summers of 1912 and 1913, that he began a long poem on the *Nibelung's Ring*. What makes the 801 lines of the unfinished poem such a remarkable achievement for a boy of 14 and 15 is that the young poet's only source was a series of synopses of Wagnerian operas published in a periodical of the gramophone trade called *Soundbox*.*

From 1913–14 Lewis was a student at Malvern College ('Wyvern' in *Surprised by Joy*). While there he kept up a correspondence with his friend Arthur Greeves, from Ulster, with whom he shared a taste for Norse mythology. In his weekly letters to Greeves he urged him to collaborate on a tragedy, Norse in subject and Greek in form. We do not know if Greeves ever attempted his share in this musical drama, but I

---

*All 801 lines are preserved in the *Lewis Papers*, vol. III, pp. 321–6. (The *Lewis Papers* consist of one set of eleven volumes of letters, diaries, and other family documents in typescript compiled by Major W. H. Lewis from original manuscripts. It is to Major Lewis, who owns the *Lewis Papers*, that I am indebted for permission to quote from them here.)

learn from Major Lewis that Lewis completed the lyric text of *Loki Bound* that occupied thirty-two pages of a folio notebook. Loki's opening speech, for which 'sombre and eerie' music is required (this was to be Greeves' contribution) begins:

> This is the awful city of the gods,
> Founded on high to overlook the world;
> And yonder gabled hall, whose golden roof
> With two fold force, is Valhall. Yonder throne
> That crowns th' eternal city's highest peak
> Is Odin's throne, whence once the impious Frey
> With ill-starred passion eyed the demon maid.*

Following his year at Malvern, Lewis was sent as a private pupil to W. T. Kirkpatrick at Great Bookham in Surrey. It was here that he wrote most of the fifty-two short poems which he later copied into a notebook under the title *Metrical Meditations of a Cod*;† most of these poems, with a few additions and alterations, being later published as *Spirits in Bondage* under the pseudonym Clive Hamilton (Heinemann, London, 1919). We learn from his letters to Greeves at this time not only of his growing interest in the Arthurian legends and the *Faerie Queene*, but that he had begun a prose romance entitled *The Quest of Bleheris*. I do not know how far he got with this story before he began— what may interest us more—a *prose* version of the Dymer story as well as a long narrative poem on *Medea's Childhood*.

Both the prose *Dymer* and *Medea* had to be put aside when Lewis went up to Oxford as a scholar of University College in April 1917. Before he had completed his first term he was recruited into the army and, after nearly six months in France, was wounded and sent home. He had continued his reading of the classics and English literature even in the trenches and, during his convalescence in an army hospital at Eastbourne, he set about preparing his *Metrical Meditations* for publication. Yet it seems his deep love for verse *and* story could only be satisfied by writing long narrative poems. Thus, while he was still at Eastbourne, he continued his old Bookham version of *Medea's Childhood*. Dissatisfied with the poem he quietly made the 300 lines he had written into spills for

---

* These are the first of 109 lines of *Loki Bound* found in the *Lewis Papers*, vol. IV, pp. 218–20.

† *Lewis Papers*, vol. IV, p. 306. 'Cod' is an expression of humorous and insincere self-depreciation.

lighting his pipe, returning with renewed interest to *Dymer*, which had now become a poem. I quote part of a letter he wrote to Arthur Greeves in December 1918, because the ideas in it strike me as being very similar to those Lewis mentions in the preface to the 1950 edition of *Dymer* printed in this book.

I have just finished a short narrative, which is a verse version of our old friend 'Dymer', greatly reduced & altered to my new ideas. The main idea is that of development by self-destruction, both of individuals & species (as man produces man only to conquer her [*sic*], & man produces a future & higher generation to conquer the ideals of the last, or again as an individual produces a nobler mood to undo all that to-day's has done). The background proceeds on the old assumption of good *outside* & *opposed to* the cosmic order. It is written in the metre of Venus and Adonis: 'Dymer' is changed to 'Ask' (you remember Ask and Embla in the Norse myths) & it is in the 3rd person under the the title of 'The Redemption of Ask'.*

In January 1919 Lewis returned to Oxford and took a First in Honour Mods. (1920), a First in Greats (1922), and a First in English (1923). All this time he was working on several narrative poems. In the Easter Vacation of 1919 he wrote to Arthur Greeves about a poem on Merlin and Nimue in blank verse as well as a new version of *Medea's Childhood*. 'The "Medea" ', he wrote to Greeves in July 1919, 'is very nearly finished, and will be about twelve hundred lines. The main interest hangs on the family relations of the horrible old king and his daughter, whom I imagine as a sort of Emily Brontë, only more of a wolf —some of her father's bad blood coming out. The defect of the poem as a whole will be—heaven help us!—dullness.' Lewis was a severe critic of his own poetry and the new *Medea* had an even shorter life than the first. In September of 1919 he wrote to Greeves saying:

I had the pleasure of looking over my 'Medea' of which I told you and finding that it was all hopeless and only fit for the fire! Nothing daunted however I bade it a long farewell—poor still-born—and

---

* A microfilm of all Lewis's letters to Arthur Greeves can be found in the Bodleian Library. On discovering two trees, the ash (Ask) and the elm (Embla), hewn into rude semblances of the human form, the Norse gods called them into life and caused them to be man and woman.

consoled myself by turning the 'Nimue' from a monologue into a narrative, in which form it will do. It appears in 'stanzas' of my own invention and is rather indebted to 'St Agnes Eve' with touches of Christabel . . . It relates the events of a single evening—Merlin coming back & catching Nimue at last.

Lewis kept a diary off and on from 1922 to 1930, and besides frequent references to other narrative poems such as *Wild Hunt, Foster, Helen,* and *Sigrid* (none of which I have ever seen or believe to be extant), I discover that *Nimue* was still 'alive' as late as April 1922. One of the most intriguing entries comes on April 2nd, 1922: 'I sat in my own bedroom by an open window and started on a poem on Dymer in rhyme royal.* We learn from Lewis's preface to the 1950 edition of *Dymer* about as much as we ever shall about the *meaning* of the poem. What we discover from his diaries is that he worked on the poem almost daily from 1922 until its original publication in 1926. His moments of satisfaction with the poem seem to be about as frequent as his moments of dissatisfaction, and he appears to have been much influenced by the advice of his friends Owen Barfield, Cecil Harwood, and Leo Baker.

The whole text of *Dymer* was in existence in April of 1924, but Lewis continued to revise lines and stanzas until he was at last satisfied. Indeed, he continued to revise the poem until and during its appearance in galley-proofs.†

As far as I know, the only manuscript of *Dymer* to escape being burnt consists of eighty-six pages of rough drafts of Cantos VI, VII, VIII, and IX which were written in one of Lewis's notebooks now in my possession. My guess is that they were composed in 1924–25 because of their close resemblance to the printed version. I have made one discovery from studying these rough drafts which I consider worth recording here. The idea of making a book end with the author waking from a dream appealed very strongly to Lewis, as can be seen from *The Pilgrim's Regress* and *The Great Divorce*. Apparently Lewis toyed with the idea of making the story of Dymer a dream, for in my manuscript of *Dymer* Lewis added one further stanza after Canto IX, 35, in which he, the dreamer, awakes.

---

* *Letters of C. S. Lewis,* Edited with a Memoir by W. H. Lewis, p. 73(1966).
† See Note 1.

Though I have never seen his poem on Helen, the daughter of Zeus and Leda became the central character in Lewis's unfinished novel *After Ten Years.* * And Merlin, with quite a different purpose than revenge on Nimue, found a significant place in *That Hideous Strength.*

Another of Lewis's novels which had its origins in verse is *Till We Have Faces*, a reinterpretation of the myth of Cupid and Psyche as told by Apuleieus. In his diary for November 23rd, 1922, he wrote: 'I went out for a walk ... thinking how to make a masque or play of Psyche and Caspian.'† Then, on September 9th, 1923, he wrote: 'My head was very full of my old idea of a poem on my version of the Cupid and Psyche story in which Psyche's sister would not be jealous, but unable to see anything but moors when Psyche showed her the palace. I have tried it twice before, once in couplet and once in ballad form.'‡ Fortunately, seventy-eight lines of the version in couplets survive.

We need a few biographical facts before we discuss the other three narrative poems in this book. On the original publication of *Dymer* in 1926 Lewis was disappointed and believed that he had unmistakably failed as a poet. His unhappiness was, however, partly counterbalanced by his election to a fellowship in English language and literature at Magdalen College, Oxford, in 1925. This meant that his future did not depend upon his being a successful poet, and with a settled income his financial worries were lightened. He was, nevertheless, disheartened because the modern world, he felt, would not make the effort to read long narrative poems. What he saw in its place was the growing popularity of the new *avant-garde* poets such as T. S. Eliot, whose poetry he could never learn to like. But, seen in perspective, all this seems of little significance beside his conversion to Christianity, which took place during the years 1929–31 and affected everything he wrote afterwards.

A few years later Lewis established himself as a scholar and writer, and, beginning with the publication of *The Allegory of Love* in 1936, he never looked back. On the other hand, nor did he ever, I think, give up hope that someone would write a narrative poem that he could add to his favourites: *The Faerie Queene, The Prelude, The Ring and the*

* This appears in Lewis's *Of Other Worlds: Essays and Stories*, ed. Walter Hooper (1966).

† *Lewis Papers*, vol. VII, p. 281.

‡ ibid., vol. VIII, p. 150.

Book, and *The Earthly Paradise.* Nor could he give up writing, primarily for his own satisfaction, short poems, some of which he published in various periodicals under the pseudonym 'Nat Whilk'.* Most of these short poems I collected after his death and published as *Poems* (Bles, London, 1964). He wrote some longer poems as well but the modern hostility to romanticism was contrary to his taste and none of these were published in his lifetime. The only ones which have survived are those published in this book.

There is little I can say of *Launcelot* except that it reflects his deep love for the 'matter of Britain' (especially Malory) and, judging from the handwriting, it was probably written in the early 1930s. It has, I think, survived simply and solely because it was written in one of the notebooks which contains some of his lecture notes on renaissance literature.

As a tutor in English literature at Magdalen College, he was required to teach his students Old English. It was, I think, because he loved the Old English alliterative line, and because he always wanted to write a long story in verse, that he composed *The Nameless Isle* (my title). This poem, which was fair-copied into a notebook and dated 'Aug. 1930', is headed by a short introduction on the alliterative line which can be found in Note 2.†

And now we come to *The Queen of Drum* which I consider, without doubt, Lewis's best poem. It has a long and interesting history and spans both his atheist and his Christian years. It is first mentioned in his diary for January 16th, 1927, where he writes: 'I ... worked on the first chunk of the King of Drum, wh. is to consist, I hope, of three short chunks—about 130 lines each. This chunk is a new version of a piece I began writing about two years ago, wh. in itself was a rewriting of the Wild Hunt (about 1920) which in its turn was based on something I started in Bristol in 1918.'‡ On January 21st, 1927, he wrote: '[I] settled down ... to the King of Drum. Produced about 20 lines for the opening of the next chunk, in a metre I have never struck before (rhythm of O.E. verse, but riming [*sic*]), with very little effort and greatly to my

---

* Old English for 'I know not whom'.

† An even better introduction is Lewis's essay 'The Alliterative Metre' in his *Selected Literary Essays,* ed. Walter Hooper (Cambridge, 1969).

‡ *Lewis Papers,* vol. IX, p. 143.

satisfaction. I also began to simmer with ideas for the further development of the story.'* Lewis mentioned the Drum story in his diary almost every day, but the next revealing entry comes on February 6th, 1927: 'I spent the morning writing, got over the King's first interview with the Queen and made a start on the "College meeting".'† Suddenly the *Queen* of Drum emerges into greater prominence, for he writes on February 27th 1927: '[I] tried desperately to re-write the Queen's speech in the Drum poem all morning without the slightest success. The old difficulty of smelting down a nasty little bit of factual stuff (the Queen's *conviction* of the others) into poetry. One only exceeds in expanding it into rhetoric.'‡

The 'something' Lewis wrote in Bristol in 1918 was, I suspect, a poem entitled *Hippolytus* about which he wrote to Arthur Greeves in September 1919. *Hippolytus* then became *Wild Hunt,* which he also wrote to Greeves about in June of 1920. Thus we move, if I am correct, from *Hippolytus* to *Wild Hunt* to the '*King* of Drum' and finally, by degrees, to the finished poem *The Queen of Drum.*

There is evidence for this. In the same notebook in which the Cupid and Psyche fragment was found, there were ninety-six lines of a poem about Hippolytus. Hippolytus was, I suspect, the hero of *Wild Hunt,* because following these ninety-six lines was the fragment of another poem told in often the same language except that Hippolytus had become the King of Drum.

My guess is that *The Queen of Drum* must date from about 1933–34 when the *Führer* of the Nazis was still a less familiar figure than the *Duce* of the Fascists. This I say because of what appears to me very convincing 'internal evidence'. I know that it was not composed later than 1938 because Lewis sent the manuscript to John Masefield for his criticism, and, though none of Masefield's letters to Lewis is dated, the envelope in which he returned the poem to Lewis is postmarked June 3rd, 1938. Masefield's letters can be found in Note 3.

Some readers may wonder what the Dymer story is about, but I do not anticipate that they will find a similar difficulty with *The Queen of Drum.* Furthermore, the author is in perfect control of his verse-medium, which

* ibid., p. 146.
† ibid., p. 155.
‡ ibid., p. 162.

[xiii]

helps him to tell his story. Besides the poem's poetical merits, I would say that *The Queen of Drum* is a Christian work, though not written from Lewis's usual objective basis: the Christianity emerges, and even the theme of Drumland (Romanticism) is developed on its own merits, and not as a Christian byway.

Dymer is the only poem in this book which has been published before: in 1926 under the pseudonym Clive Hamilton, and in 1950 under the author's own name. *Launcelot* and *The Nameless Isle* were in Lewis's handwriting, and *The Queen of Drum* in typescript. Because Lewis did not prepare the last three poems for publication, I have taken the liberty of correcting errors in spelling and punctuation. Trusting that they will prove of interest to some readers, I have preserved all the author's alternative readings, which are printed in the footnotes.

I am grateful to J. M. Dent & Sons Ltd for permission to reprint *Dymer,* and to Major W. H. Lewis and the Trustees of C. S. Lewis's Estate for allowing me to publish the other poems in this book. I wish also to express my gratitude to The Society of Authors as the literary representative of the Estate of John Masefield for permission to publish his letters to Lewis. It is a pleasure to name publicly my friends Dr and Mrs Austin Farrer, Mr Roger Lancelyn Green, Mr Owen Barfield, Professor John Lawlor, and Mr Spiros-Sitaridis, who, by their encouragement and wise advice, helped me in editing these poems.

WALTER HOOPER

Jesus College, Oxford
May 1969

DYMER

PREFACE BY THE AUTHOR
TO THE 1950 EDITION

At its original appearance in 1926, *Dymer*, like many better books, found some good reviews and almost no readers. The idea of disturbing its repose in the grave now comes from its publishers, not from me, but I have a reason for wishing to be present at the exhumation. Nearly a quarter of a century has gone since I wrote it, and in that time things have changed both within me and round me; my old poem might be misunderstood by those who now read it for the first time.

I am told that the Persian poets draw a distinction between poetry which they have 'found' and poetry which they have 'brought': if you like, between the given and the invented, though they wisely refuse to identify this with the distinction between good and bad. Their terminology applies with unusual clarity to my poem. What I 'found', what simply 'came to me', was the story of a man who, on some mysterious bride, begets a monster: which monster, as soon as it has killed its father, becomes a god. This story arrived, complete, in my mind somewhere about my seventeenth year. To the best of my knowledge I did not consciously or voluntarily invent it, nor was it, in the plain sense of that word, a dream. All I know about it is that there was a time when it was not there, and then presently a time when it was. Every one may allegorise it or psychoanalyse it as he pleases: and if I did so myself my interpretations would have no more authority than anyone else's.

The Platonic and totalitarian state from which Dymer escapes in Canto I was a natural invention for one who detested the state in Plato's *Republic* as much as he liked everything else in Plato, and who was, by temperament, an extreme anarchist. I put into it my hatred of my public school and my recent hatred of the army. But I was already critical of my own anarchism. There had been a time when the sense of defiant and almost drunken liberation which fills the first two acts of *Siegfried* had completely satisfied me. Now, I thought, I knew better. My hero therefore must go through his Siegfried moment in Cantos I and II and

[3]

find in Canto IV what really comes of that mood in the end. For it seemed to me that two opposite forces in man tended equally to revolt. The one criticises and at need defies civilisation because it is not good enough, the other stabs it from below and behind because it is already too good for total baseness to endure. The hero who dethrones a tyrant will therefore be first fêted and afterwards murdered by the rabble who feel a disinterested hatred of order and reason as such. Hence, in Canto IV, Bran's revolt which at once parodies and punishes Dymer's. It will be remembered that, when I wrote, the first horrors of the Russian Revolution were still fresh in every one's mind; and in my own country, Ulster, we had had opportunities of observing the daemonic character of popular political 'causes'.

In those days the new psychology was just beginning to make itself felt in the circles I most frequented at Oxford. This joined forces with the fact that we felt ourselves (as young men always do) to be escaping from the illusions of adolescence, and as a result we were much exercised about the problem of fantasy or wishful thinking. The 'Christiana Dream', as we called it (after Christiana Pontifex in Butler's novel), was the hidden enemy whom we were all determined to unmask and defeat. My hero, therefore, had to be a man who had succumbed to its allurements and finally got the better of them. But the particular form in which this was worked out depended on two peculiarities of my own history.

(1) From at least the age of six, romantic longing—*Sehnsucht*—had played an unusually central part in my experience. Such longing is in itself the very reverse of wishful thinking: it is more like thoughtful wishing. But it throws off what may be called systems of imagery. One among many such which it had thrown off for me was the Hesperian or Western Garden system, mainly derived from Euripides, Milton, Morris, and the early Yeats. By the time I wrote *Dymer* I had come, under the the influence of our common obsession about Christiana Dreams, into a state of angry revolt against that spell. I regarded it as the very type of the illusions I was trying to escape from. It must therefore be savagely attacked. Dymer's temptation to relapse into the world of fantasy therefore comes to him (Canto VII) in that form. All through that canto I am cutting down my own former 'groves and high places' and biting the hand that had fed me. I even tried to get the sneer into the metre; the archaic spelling and accentuation of *countrie* in vii. 23 is

meant as parody. In all this, as I now believe, I was mistaken. Instead of repenting my idolatry I spat upon the images which only my own mis-understanding greed had ever made into idols. But 'the heresies that men leave are hated most' and lovers' quarrels can be the bitterest of all.

(2) Several years before I wrote the poem, back in my teens, when my mind, except for a vigilant rejection of Christianity, had no fixed prin-ciples, and everything from strict materialism to theosophy could find by turns an entry, I had been, as boys are, temporarily attracted to what what was then called 'the Occult'. I blundered into it innocently enough. In those days every one was reading Maeterlinck, and I wanted to im-prove my French. Moreover, from Yeats's early poetry it was natural to turn to his prose; and there I found to my astonishment that Yeats, unlike other romantic poets, really and literally believed in the sort of beings he put into his poems. There was no question here of 'symbolism': he believed in magic. And so for a time *Rosa Alchemica* took its turn (along with Voltaire, Lucretius, and Joseph McCabe) among my serious books. You will understand that this period had ended a long time (years are longer at that age) before I set about writing *Dymer*. By then, so far as I was anything, I was an idealist, and for an idealist all super-naturalisms were equally illusions, all 'spirits' merely symbols of 'Spirit' in the metaphysical sense, futile and dangerous if mistaken for facts. I put this into vii. 8. I was now quite sure that magic or spiritism of any kind was a fantasy and of all fantasies the worst. But this wholesome conviction had recently been inflamed into a violent antipathy. It had happened to me to see a man, and a man whom I loved, sink into screaming mania and finally into death under the influence, as I be-lieved, of spiritualism. And I had also been twice admitted to the upper room in Yeats's own house in Broad Street. His conversation turned much on magic. I was overawed by his personality, and by his doctrine half fascinated and half repelled because of the fascination.

The angel in the last canto does not of course mean that I had any Christian beliefs when I wrote the poem, any more (*si parva licet com-ponere magnis*) than the conclusion of *Faust*, Part II, means that Goethe was a believer.

This, I think, explains all that the reader might want explained in my narrative. My hero was to be a man escaping from illusion. He begins by egregiously supposing the universe to be his friend and seems for a time to find confirmation of his belief. Then he tries, as we all try, to repeat his moment of youthful rapture. It cannot be done; the old Matriarch sees to that. On top of his rebuff comes the discovery of the consequences which his rebellion against the City has produced. He sinks into despair and gives utterance to the pessimism which had, on the whole, been my own view about six years earlier. Hunger and a shock of real danger bring him to his senses and he at last accepts reality. But just as he is setting out on the new and soberer life, the shabbiest of all brides is offered him; the false promise that by magic or invited illusion there may be a short cut back to the one happiness he remembers. He relapses and swallows the bait, but he has grown too mature to be really deceived. He finds that the wish-fulfilment dream leads to the fear-fulfilment dream, recovers himself, defies the Magician who tempted him, and faces his destiny.

The physical appearance of the Magician in vi. 6–9 owes something to Yeats as I saw him. If he were now alive I would ask his pardon with shame for having repaid his hospitality by such freedom. It was not done in malice, and the likeness is not, I think, in itself, uncomplimentary.

Since his great name here comes before us, let me take the opportunity of saluting his genius: a genius so potent that, having first revivified and transmuted that romantic tradition which he found almost on its death-bed (and invented a new kind of blank verse in the process), he could then go on to weather one of the bitterest literary revolutions we have known, embark on a second career, and, as it were with one hand, play most of the moderns off the field at their own game. If there is, as may be thought, a pride verging on insolence in his later work, such pride has never come so near to being excusable. It must have been difficult for him to respect either the mere Romantics who could only bewail a lost leader or the mere moderns who could see no difference between *On Baile's Strand* and the work of Richard le Gallienne.

Some may be surprised at the strength of the anti-totalitarian feeling in a poem written so long ago. I had not read *Brave New World* or *Land Under England* or *The Aerodrome*: nor had we yet tasted the fruits of a planned economy in our own lives. This should be a warning for critics who attempt to date ancient texts too exactly on that kind of internal evidence.

1950   C.S.L.

CANTO I

1

You stranger, long before your glance can light
Upon these words, time will have washed away
The moment when I first took pen to write,
With all my road before me—yet to-day,
Here, if at all, we meet; the unfashioned clay
Ready to both our hands; both hushed to see
That which is nowhere yet come forth and be.

2

This moment, if you join me, we begin
A partnership where both must toil to hold
The clue that I caught first. We lose or win
Together; if you read, you are enrolled.
And first, a marvel—Who could have foretold
That in the city which men called in scorn
The Perfect City, Dymer could be born?

3

There you'd have thought the gods were smothered down
Forever, and the keys were turned on fate.
No hour was left unchartered in that town,
And love was in a schedule and the State
Chose for eugenic reasons who should mate
With whom, and when. Each idle song and dance
Was fixed by law and nothing left to chance.

4

For some of the last Platonists had founded
That city of old. And masterly they made
An island of what ought to be, surrounded
By this gross world of easier light and shade.
All answering to the master's dream they laid
The strong foundations, torturing into stone
Each bubble that the Academy had blown.

5

This people were so pure, so law-abiding,
So logical, they made the heavens afraid:
They sent the very swallows into hiding
By their appalling chastity dismayed:
More soberly the lambs in spring-time played
Because of them: and ghosts dissolved in shame
Before their common-sense—till Dymer came.

6

At Dymer's birth no comets scared the nation,
The public crêche engulfed him with the rest,
And twenty separate Boards of Education
Closed round him. He passed through every test,
Was vaccinated, numbered, washed and dressed,
Proctored, inspected, whipt, examined weekly,
And for some nineteen years he bore it meekly.

7

For nineteen years they worked upon his soul,
Refining, chipping, moulding and adorning.
Then came the moment that undid the whole—
The ripple of rude life without a warning.

It came in lecture-time one April morning
—Alas for laws and locks, reproach and praise,
Who ever learned to censor the spring days?

8

A little breeze came stirring to his cheek.
He looked up to the window. A brown bird
Perched on the sill, bent down to whet his beak
With darting head—Poor Dymer watched and stirred
Uneasily. The lecturer's voice he heard
Still droning from the dais. The narrow room
Was drowsy, over-solemn, filled with gloom.

9

He yawned, and a voluptuous laziness
Tingled down all his spine and loosed his knees,
Slow-drawn, like an invisible caress.
He laughed—The lecturer stopped like one that sees
A Ghost, then frowned and murmured, 'Silence, please.'
That moment saw the soul of Dymer hang
In the balance—Louder then his laughter rang.

10

The whole room watched with unbelieving awe.
He rose and staggered rising. From his lips
Broke yet again the idiot-like guffaw.
He felt the spirit in his finger-tips,
Then swinging his right arm—a wide ellipse
Yet lazily—he struck the lecturer's head.
The old man tittered, lurched and dropt down dead.

11

Out of the silent room, out of the dark
Into the sun-stream Dymer passed, and there
The sudden breezes, the high-hanging lark,

[9]

The milk-white clouds sailing in polished air,
Suddenly flashed about him like a blare
Of trumpets. And no cry was raised behind him,
His class sat dazed. They dared not go to find him.

12

Yet wonderfully some rumour spread abroad—
An inarticulate sense of life renewing
In each young heart—He whistled down the road:
Men said: 'There's Dymer'—'Why, what's Dymer doing?'
'I don't know'—'Look, there's Dymer,'—far pursuing
With troubled eyes—A long mysterious 'Oh'
Sighed from a hundred throats to see him go.

13

Down the white street and past the gate and forth
Beyond the wall he came to grassy places.
There was a shifting wind to West and North,
With clouds in heeling squadron running races.
The shadows following on the sunlight's traces
Crossed the whole field and each wild flower within it
With change of wavering glories every minute.

14

There was a river, flushed with rains, between
The flat fields and a forest's willowy edge.
A sauntering pace he shuffled on the green,
He kicked his boots against the crackly sedge
And tore his hands in many a furzy hedge.
He saw his feet and ankles gilded round
With buttercups that carpeted the ground.

He looked back then. The line of a low hill
Had hid the city's towers and domes from sight;
He stopt: he felt a break of sunlight spill
Around him sudden waves of searching light.
Upon the earth was green, and gold, and white,
Smothering his feet. He felt his city dress
An insult to that April cheerfulness.

16

He said: 'I've worn this dustheap long enough;
Here goes!' And forthwith in the open field
He stripped away that prison of sad stuff:
Socks, jacket, shirt and breeches off he peeled
And rose up mother-naked with no shield
Against the sun: then stood awhile to play
With bare toes dabbling in cold river clay.

17

Forward again, and sometimes leaping high
With arms outspread as though he would embrace
In one act all the circle of the sky:
Sometimes he rested in a leafier place,
And crushed the wet, cool flowers against his face:
And once he cried aloud, 'O world, O day,
Let, let me,'—and then found no prayer to say.

18

Up furrows still unpierced with earliest crop
He marched. Through woods he strolled from flower to flower,
And over hills. As ointment drop by drop

[11]

Preciously meted out, so hour by hour
The day slipped through his hands: and now the power
Failed in his feet from walking. He was done,
Hungry and cold. That moment sank the sun.

19

He lingered—Looking up, he saw ahead
The black and bristling frontage of a wood,
And over it the large sky swimming red,
Freckled with homeward crows. Surprised he stood
To feel that wideness quenching his hot mood,
Then shouted, 'Trembling darkness, trembling green,
What do you mean, wild wood, what do you mean?'

20

He shouted. But the solitude received
His noise into her noiselessness, his fire
Into her calm. Perhaps he half believed
Some answer yet would come to his desire.
The hushed air quivered softly like a wire
Upon his voice. It echoed, it was gone:
The quiet and the quiet dark went on.

21

He rushed into the wood. He struck and stumbled
On hidden roots. He groped and scratched his face.
The little birds woke chattering where he fumbled.
The stray cat stood, paw lifted, in mid-chase.
There is a windless calm in such a place:
A sense of being indoors—so crowded stand
The living trees, watching on every hand:

A sense of trespass—such as in the hall
Of the wrong house, one time, to me befell.
Groping between the hat-stand and the wall—
A clear voice from above me like a bell,
The sweet voice of a woman asking 'Well?'
No more than this. And as I fled I wondered
Into whose alien story I had blundered.

23

A like thing fell to Dymer. Bending low,
Feeling his way he went. The curtained air
Sighed into sound above his head, as though
Stringed instruments and horns were riding there.
It passed and at its passing stirred his hair.
He stood intent to hear. He heard again
And checked his breath half-drawn, as if with pain.

24

That music could have crumbled proud belief
With doubt, or in the bosom of the sage
Madden the heart that had outmastered grief,
And flood with tears the eyes of frozen age
And turn the young man's feet to pilgrimage—
So sharp it was, so sure a path it found,
Soulward with stabbing wounds of bitter sound.

25

It died out on the middle of a note,
As though it failed at the urge of its own meaning.
It left him with life quivering at the throat,
Limbs shaken and wet cheeks and body leaning,

With strain towards the sound and senses gleaning
The last, least, ebbing ripple of the air,
Searching the emptied darkness, muttering 'Where?'

26

Then followed such a time as is forgotten
With morning light, but in the passing seems
Unending. Where he grasped the branch was rotten,
Where he trod forth in haste the forest streams
Laid wait for him. Like men in fever dreams
Climbing an endless rope, he laboured much
And gained no ground. He reached and could not touch.

27

And often out of darkness like a swell
That grows up from no wind upon blue sea,
He heard the music, unendurable
In stealing sweetness wind from tree to tree.
Battered and bruised in body and soul was he
When first he saw a little lightness growing
Ahead: and from that light the sound was flowing.

28

The trees were fewer now: and gladly nearing
That light, he saw the stars. For sky was there,
And smoother grass, white-flowered—a forest clearing
Set in seven miles of forest, secreter
Than valleys in the tops of clouds, more fair
Than greenery under snow or desert water,
Or the white peace descending after slaughter.

29

As some who have been wounded beyond healing
Wake, or half wake, once only and so bless,
Far off the lamplight travelling on the ceiling,

A disk of pale light filled with peacefulness,
And wonder if this is the C.C.S.,
Or home, or heaven, or dreams—then sighing win
Wise, ignorant death before the pains begin:

30

So Dymer in the wood-lawn blessed the light,
A still light, rosy, clear, and filled with sound.
Here was some pile of building which the night
Made larger. Spiry shadows rose all round,
But through the open door appeared profound
Recesses of pure light—fire with no flame—
And out of that deep light the music came.

31

Tip-toes he slunk towards it where the grass
Was twinkling in a lane of light before
The archway. There was neither fence to pass
Nor word of challenge given, nor bolted door;
But where it's open, open evermore,
No knocker and no porter and no guard,
For very strangeness entering in grows hard.

32

Breathe not! Speak not! Walk gently. Someone's here.
Why have they left their house with the door so wide?
There must be someone. . . . Dymer hung in fear
Upon the threshold, longing and big-eyed.
At last he squared his shoulders, smote his side
And called, 'I'm here. Now let the feast begin.
I'm coming now. I'm Dymer,' and went in.

CANTO II

1

More light. Another step, and still more light
Opening ahead. It swilled with soft excess
His eyes yet quivering from the dregs of night,
And it was nowhere more and nowhere less:
In it no shadows were. He could not guess
Its fountain. Wondering round around he turned:
Still on each side the level glory burned.

2

Far in the dome to where his gaze was lost
The deepening roof shone clear as stones that lie
In-shore beneath pure seas. The aisles, that crossed
Like forests of white stone their arms on high,
Past pillar after pillar dragged his eye
In unobscured perspective, till the sight
Was weary. And there also was the light.

3

Look with my eyes. Conceive yourself above
And hanging in the dome: and thence through space
Look down. See Dymer, dwarfed and naked, move,
A white blot on the floor, at such a pace
As boats that hardly seem to have changed place
Once in an hour when from the cliffs we spy
The same ship always smoking towards the sky.

4

The shouting mood had withered from his heart;
The oppression of huge places wrapped him round.
A great misgiving sent its fluttering dart
Deep into him—some fear of being found,
Some hope to find he knew not what. The sound
Of music, never ceasing, took the rôle
Of silence and like silence numbed his soul.

5

Till, as he turned a corner, his deep awe
Broke with a sudden start. For straight ahead,
Far off, a wild-eyed, naked man he saw
That came to meet him: and beyond was spread
Yet further depth of light. With quickening tread
He leaped towards the shape. Then stooped and smiled
Before a mirror, wondering like a child.

6

Beside the glass, unguarded, for the claiming,
Like a great patch of flowers upon the wall
Hung every kind of clothes: silk, feathers flaming,
Leopard skin, furry mantles like the fall
Of deep mid-winter snows. Upon them all
Hung the faint smell of cedar, and the dyes
Were bright as blood and clear as morning skies.

7

He turned from the white spectre in the glass
And looked at these. Remember, he had worn
Thro' winter slush, thro' summer flowers and grass
One kind of solemn stuff since he was born,

With badge of year and rank. He laughed in scorn
And cried, 'Here is no law, nor eye to see,
Nor leave of entry given. Why should there be?

8

'Have done with that—you threw it all behind.
Henceforth I ask no licence where I need.
It's on, on, on, though I go mad and blind,
Though knees ache and lungs labour and feet bleed,
Or else—it's home again: to sleep and feed,
And work, and hate them always and obey
And loathe the punctual rise of each new day.'

9

He made mad work among them as he dressed,
With motley choice and litter on the floor,
And each thing as he found it seemed the best.
He wondered that he had not known before
How fair a man he was. 'I'll creep no more
In secret,' Dymer said. 'But I'll go back
And drive them all to freedom on this track.'

10

He turned towards the glass. The space looked smaller
Behind him now. Himself in royal guise
Filled the whole frame—a nobler shape and taller,
Till suddenly he started with surprise,
Catching, by chance, his own familiar eyes,
Fevered, yet still the same, without their share
Of bravery, undeceived and watching there.

11

Yet, as he turned, he cried, 'The rest remain. . . .
If they rebelled . . . if they should find me here,

We'd pluck the whole taut fabric from the strain,
Hew down the city, let live earth appear!
—Old men and barren women whom through fear
We have suffered to be masters in our home,
Hide! hide! for we are angry and we come.'

12

Thus feeding on vain fancy, covering round
His hunger, his great loneliness arraying
In facile dreams until the qualm was drowned,
The boy went on. Through endless arches straying
With casual tread he sauntered, manly playing
At manhood lest more loss of faith betide him,
Till lo! he saw a table set beside him.

13

When Dymer saw this sight, he leaped for mirth,
He clapped his hands, his eye lit like a lover's.
He had a hunger in him that was worth
Ten cities. Here was silver, glass and covers.
Cold peacock, prawns in aspic, eggs of plovers,
Raised pies that stood like castles, gleaming fishes
And bright fruit with broad leaves around the dishes.

14

If ever you have passed a café door
And lingered in the dusk of a June day,
Fresh from the road, sweat-sodden and foot-sore,
And heard the plates clink and the music play,
With laughter, with white tables far away,
With many lights—conceive how Dymer ran
To table, looked once round him, and began.

That table seemed unending. Here and there
Were broken meats, bread crumbled, flowers defaced
—A napkin, with white petals, on a chair,
—A glass already tasted, still to taste.
It seemed that a great host had fed in haste
And gone: yet left a thousand places more
Untouched, wherein no guest had sat before.

16

There in the lonely splendour Dymer ate,
As thieves eat, ever watching, half in fear.
He blamed his evil fortune. 'I come late.
Whose board was this? What company sat here?
What women with wise mouths, what comrades dear
Who would have made me welcome as the one
Free-born of all my race and cried, Well, done!'

17

Remember, yet again, he had grown up
On rations and on scientific food,
At common boards, with water in his cup,
One mess alike for every day and mood:
But here, at his right hand, a flagon stood.
He raised it, paused before he drank, and laughed.
'I'll drown their Perfect City in this draught.'

18

He fingered the cold neck. He saw within,
Like a strange sky, some liquor that foamed blue

And murmured. Standing now with pointed chin
And head thrown back, he tasted. Rapture flew
Through every vein. That moment louder grew
The music and swelled forth a trumpet note.
He ceased and put one hand up to his throat.

19

Then heedlessly he let the flagon sink
In his right hand. His staring eyes were caught
In distance, as of one who tries to think
A thought that is still waiting to be thought.
There was a riot in his heart that brought
The loud blood to the temples. A great voice
Sprang to his lips unsummoned, with no choice.

20

'Ah! but the eyes are open, the dream is broken!
To sack the Perfect City? . . . a fool's deed
For Dymer! Folly of follies I have spoken!
I am the wanderer, new born, newly freed . . .
A thousand times they have warned me of men's greed
For joy, for the good that all desire, but never
Till now I knew the wild heat of the endeavour.

21

'Some day I will come back to break the City,
—Not now. Perhaps when age is white and bleak
—Not now. I am in haste. O God, the pity
Of all my life till this, groping and weak,
The shadow of itself! But now to seek
That true most ancient glory whose white glance
Was lost through the whole world by evil chance!

'I was a dull, cowed thing from the beginning.
Dymer the drudge, the blackleg who obeyed.
Desire shall teach me now. If this be sinning,
Good luck to it! O splendour long delayed,
Beautiful world of mine, O world arrayed
For bridal, flower and forest, wave and field,
I come to be your lover. Loveliest, yield!

23

'World, I will prove you. Lest it should be said
There was man who loved the earth: his heart
Was nothing but that love. With doting tread
He worshipt the loved grass: and every start
Of every bird from cover, the least part
Of every flower he held in awe. Yet earth
Gave him no joy between his death and birth.

24

'I know my good is hidden at your breast.
There is a sound of great good in my ear,
Like wings. And, oh! this moment is the best;
I shall not fail—I taste it—it comes near.
As men from a dark dungeon see the clear
Stars shining and the filled streams far away,
I hear your promise booming and obey.

25

'This forest lies a thousand miles, perhaps,
Beyond where I am come. And farther still
The rivers wander seaward with smooth lapse,
And there is cliff and cottage, tower and hill.

Somewhere, before the world's end, I shall fill
My spirit at earth's pap. For earth must hold
One rich thing sealed as Dymer's from of old.

26

'One rich thing—or, it may be, more than this . . .
Might I not reach the borders of a land
That ought to have been mine? And there, the bliss
Of free speech, there the eyes that understand,
The men free grown, not modelled by the hand
Of masters—men that know, or men that seek,
—They will not gape and murmur when I speak.'

27

Then, as he ceased, amid the farther wall
He saw a curtained and low lintelled door;
—Dark curtains, sweepy fold, night-purple pall,
He thought he had not noticed it before.
Sudden desire for darkness overbore
His will, and drew him towards it. All was blind
Within. He passed. The curtains closed behind.

28

He entered in a void. Night-scented flowers
Breathed there, but this was darker than the night
That is most black with beating thunder-showers,
—A disembodied world where depth and height
And distance were unmade. No seam of light
Showed through. It was a world not made for seeing,
One pure, one undivided sense of being.

Through darkness smooth as amber, warily, slowly
He moved. The floor was soft beneath his feet.
A cool smell that was holy and unholy,
Sharp like the very spring and roughly sweet,
Blew towards him: and he felt his fingers meet
Broad leaves and wiry stems that at his will
Unclosed before and closed behind him still.

With body intent he felt the foliage quiver
On breast and thighs. With groping arms he made
Wide passes in the air. A sacred shiver
Of joy from the heart's centre oddly strayed
To every nerve. Deep sighing, much afraid,
Much wondering, he went on: then, stooping, found
A knee-depth of warm pillows on the ground.

And there it was sweet rapture to lie still,
Eyes open on the dark. A flowing health
Bathed him from head to foot and great goodwill
Rose springing in his heart and poured its wealth
Outwards. Then came a hand as if by stealth
Out of the dark and touched his hand: and after
The beating silence budded into laughter:

—A low grave laugh and rounded like a pearl,
Mysterious, filled with home. He opened wide
His arms. The breathing body of a girl
Slid into them. From the world's end, with the stride

Of seven-leagued boots came passion to his side.
Then, meeting mouths, soft-falling hair, a cry,
Heart-shaken flank, sudden cool-folded thigh:

33

The same night swelled the mushroom in earth's lap
And silvered the wet fields: it drew the bud
From hiding and led on the rhythmic sap
And sent the young wolves thirsting after blood,
And, wheeling the big seas, made ebb and flood
Along the shores of earth: and held these two
In dead sleep till the time of morning dew.

CANTO III

1

He woke, and all at once before his eyes
The pale spires of the chestnut-trees in bloom
Rose waving and, beyond, dove-coloured skies;
But where he lay was dark and, out of gloom,
He saw them, through the doorway of a room
Full of strange scents and softness, padded deep
With growing leaves, heavy with last night's sleep.

2

He rubbed his eyes. He felt that chamber wreathing
New sleepiness around him. At his side
He was aware of warmth and quiet breathing.
Twice he sank back, loose-limbed and drowsy-eyed;
But the wind came even there. A sparrow cried
And the wood shone without. Then Dymer rose,
—'Just for one glance,' he said, and went, tip-toes,

3

Out into crisp grey air and drenching grass.
The whitened cobweb sparkling in its place
Clung to his feet. He saw the wagtail pass
Beside him and the thrush: and from his face
Felt the thin-scented winds divinely chase
The flush of sleep. Far off he saw, between
The trees, long morning shadows of dark green.

4

He stretched his lazy arms to their full height,
Yawning, and sighed and laughed, and sighed anew;
Then wandered farther, watching with delight
How his broad naked footprints stained the dew,
—Pressing his foot to feel the cold come through
Between the spreading toes—then wheeled round
Each moment to some new, shrill forest sound.

5

The wood with its cold flowers had nothing there
More beautiful than he, new waked from sleep,
New born from joy. His soul lay very bare
That moment to life's touch, and pondering deep
Now first he knew that no desire could keep
These hours for always, and that men do die
—But oh, the present glory of lungs and eye!

6

He thought: 'At home they are waking now. The stair
Is filled with feet. The bells clang—far from me.
Where am I now? I could not point to where
The City lies from here,' . . . then, suddenly,
'If I were here alone, these woods could be
A frightful place! But now I have met my friend
Who loves me, we can talk to the road's end.'

7

Thus, quickening with the sweetness of the tale
Of his new love, he turned. He saw, between
The young leaves, where the palace walls showed pale

With chilly stone: but far above the green,
Springing like cliffs in air, the towers were seen,
Making more quiet yet the quiet dawn.
Thither he came. He reached the open lawn.

8

No bird was moving here. Against the wall
Out of the unscythed grass the nettle grew.
The doors stood open wide, but no footfall
Rang in the colonnades. Whispering through
Arches and hollow halls the light wind blew . . .
His awe returned. He whistled—then, no more,
It's better to plunge in by the first door.

9

But then the vastness threw him into doubt.
Was this the door that he had found last night?
Or that, beneath the tower? Had he come out
This side at all? As the first snow falls light
With following rain before the year grows white,
So the first, dim foreboding touched his mind,
Gently as yet, and easily thrust behind.

10

And with it came the thought, 'I do not know
Her name—no, nor her face.' But still his mood
Ran blithely as he felt the morning blow
About him, and the earth-smell in the wood
Seemed waking for long hours that must be good
Here, in the unfettered lands, that knew no cause
For grudging—out of reach of the old laws.

He hastened to one entry. Up the stair,
Beneath the pillared porch, without delay,
He ran—then halted suddenly: for there
Across the quiet threshold something lay,
A bundle, a dark mass that barred the way.
He looked again, and lo, the formless pile
Under his eyes was moving all the while.

12

And it had hands, pale hands of wrinkled flesh,
Puckered and gnarled with vast antiquity,
That moved. He eyed the sprawling thing afresh,
And bit by bit (so faces come to be
In the red coal) yet surely, he could see
That the swathed hugeness was uncleanly human,
A living thing, the likeness of a woman.

13

In the centre a draped hummock marked the head;
Thence flowed the broader lines with curve and fold
Spreading as oak roots do. You would have said
A man could hide among them and grow old
In finding a way out. Breast manifold
As of the Ephesian Artemis might be
Under that robe. The face he did not see.

14

And all his being answered, 'Not that way!'
Never a word he spoke. Stealthily creeping
Back from the door he drew. Quick! No delay!

Quick, quick, but very quiet!—backward peeping
Till fairly out of sight. Then shouting, leaping,
Shaking himself, he ran—as puppies do
From bathing—till that door was out of view.

15

Another gate—and empty. In he went
And found a courtyard open to the sky,
Amidst it dripped a fountain. Heavy scent
Of flowers was here; the foxglove standing high
Sheltered the whining wasp. With hasty eye
He travelled round the walls. One doorway led
Within: one showed a further court ahead.

16

He ran up to the first—a hungry lover,
And not yet taught to endure, not blunted yet,
But weary of long waiting to discover
That loved one's face. Before his foot was set
On the first stair, he felt the sudden sweat
Cold on his sides. That sprawling mass in view,
That shape—the horror of heaviness—here too.

17

He fell back from the porch. Not yet—not yet—
There must be other ways where he would meet
No watcher in the door. He would not let
The fear rise, nor hope falter, nor defeat
Be entered in his thoughts. A sultry heat
Seemed to have filled the day. His breath came short,
And he passed on into that inner court.

And (like a dream) the sight he feared to find
Was waiting here. Then cloister, path and square
He hastened through: down paths that ended blind,
Traced and retraced his steps. The thing sat there
In every door, still watching, everywhere,
Behind, ahead, all round—So! Steady now,
Lest panic comes. He stopped. He wiped his brow.

19

But, as he strove to rally, came the thought
That he had dreamed of such a place before
—Knew how it all would end. He must be caught
Early or late. No good! But all the more
He raged with passionate will that overbore
That knowledge: and cried out, and beat his head,
Raving, upon the senseless walls, and said:

20

'Where? Where? Dear, look once out. Give but one sign.
It's I, I, Dymer. Are you chained and hidden?
What have they done to her? Loose her! She is mine.
Through stone and iron, haunted and hag-ridden,
I'll come to you—no stranger, nor unbidden,
It's I. Don't fear them. Shout above them all.
Can you not hear? I'll follow at your call.'

21

From every arch the echo of his cry
Returned. Then all was silent, and he knew
There was no other way. He must pass by

That horror: tread her down, force his way through,
Or die upon the threshold. And this too
Had all been in a dream. He felt his heart
Beating as if his throat would burst apart.

22

There was no other way. He stood a space
And pondered it. Then, gathering up his will,
He went to the next door. The pillared place
Beneath the porch was dark. The air was still,
Moss on the steps. He felt her presence fill
The threshold with dull life. Here too was she.
This time he raised his eyes and dared to see.

23

Pah! Only an old woman! . . . but the size,
The old, old matriarchal dreadfulness,
Immovable, intolerable . . . the eyes
Hidden, the hidden head, the winding dress,
Corpselike . . . The weight of the brute that seemed to press
Upon his heart and breathing. Then he heard
His own voice, strange and humbled, take the word.

24

'Good Mother, let me pass. I have a friend
To look for in this house. I slept the night
And feasted here—it was my journey's end,
—I found it by the music and the light,
And no one kept the doors, and I did right
To enter—did I not? Now, Mother, pray,
Let me pass in . . . good Mother, give me way.'

The woman answered nothing: but he saw
The hands, like crabs, still wandering on her knee.
'Mother, if I have broken any law,
I'll ask a pardon once: then let it be,
—Once is enough—and leave the passage free.
I am in haste. And though it were a sin
By all the laws you have, I must go in.'

Courage was rising in him now. He said,
'Out of my path, old woman. For this cause
I am new born, new freed, and here new wed,
That I might be the breaker of bad laws.
The frost of old forbiddings breaks and thaws
Wherever my feet fall. I bring to birth
Under its crust the green, ungrudging earth.'

He had started, bowing low: but now he stood
Stretched to his height. His own voice in his breast
Made misery pompous, firing all his blood.
'Enough,' he cried. 'Give place. You shall not wrest
My love from me. I journey on a quest
You cannot understand, whose strength shall bear me
Through fire and earth. A bogy will not scare me.

'I am the sword of spring; I am the truth.
Old night, put out your stars, the dawn is here,
The sleeper's wakening, and the wings of youth.
With crumbling veneration and cowed fear

I make no truce. My loved one, live and dear,
Waits for me. Let me in! I fled the City,
Shall I fear you or . . . Mother, ah, for pity.'

29

For his high mood fell shattered. Like a man
Unnerved, in bayonet-fighting, in the thick,
—Full of red rum and cheers when he began,
Now, in a dream, muttering: 'I've not the trick.
It's no good. I'm no good. They're all too quick.
There! Look there! Look at that!'—so Dymer stood,
Suddenly drained of hope. It was no good.

30

He pleaded then. Shame beneath shame. 'Forgive.
It may be there are powers I cannot break.
If you are of them, speak. Speak. Let me live.
I ask so small a thing. I beg. I make
My body a living prayer whose force would shake
The mountains. I'll recant—confess my sin—
But this once let me pass. I must go in.'

31

'Yield but one inch, once only from your law;
Set any price—I will give all, obey
All else but this, hold your least word in awe,
Give you no cause for anger from this day.
Answer! The least things living when they pray
As I pray now bear witness. They speak true
Against God. Answer! Mother, let me through.'

Then when he heard no answer, mad with fear
And with desire, too strained with both to know
What he desired or feared, yet staggering near,
He forced himself towards her and bent low
For grappling. Then came darkness. Then a blow
Fell on his heart, he thought. There came a blank
Of all things. As the dead sink, down he sank.

33

The first big drops are rattling on the trees,
The sky is copper dark, low thunder pealing.
See Dymer with drooped head and knocking knees
Comes from the porch. Then slowly, drunkly reeling,
Blind, beaten, broken, past desire of healing,
Past knowledge of his misery, he goes on
Under the first dark trees and now is gone.

CANTO IV

1

First came the peal that split the heavens apart
Straight overhead. Then silence. Then the rain;
Twelve miles of downward water like one dart,
And in one leap were launched along the plain,
To break the budding flower and flood the grain,
And keep with dripping sound an undersong
Amid the wheeling thunder all night long.

2

He put his hands before his face. He stooped,
Blind with his hair. The loud drops' grim tattoo
Beat him to earth. Like summer grass he drooped,
Amazed, while sheeted lightning large and blue
Blinked wide and pricked the quivering eyeball through.
Then, scrambling to his feet, with downward head
He fought into the tempest as chance led.

3

The wood was mad. Soughing of branch and straining
Was there: drumming of water. Light was none,
Nor knowledge of himself. The trees' complaining
And his own throbbing heart seemed mixed in one,
One sense of bitter loss and beauty undone;
All else was blur and chaos and rain-stream
And noise and the confusion of a dream.

4

Aha! . . . Earth hates a miserable man:
Against him even the clouds and winds conspire.
Heaven's voice smote Dymer's ear-drum as he ran,
Its red throat plagued the dark with corded fire
—Barbed flame, coiled flame that ran like living wire
Charged with disastrous current, left and right
About his path, hell-blue or staring white.

5

Stab! Stab! Blast all at once. What's he to fear?
Look there—that cedar shrivelling in swift blight
Even where he stood! And there—ah, that came near!
Oh, if some shaft would break his soul outright,
What ease so to unload and scatter quite
On the darkness this wild beating in his skull
Too burning to endure, too tense and full.

6

All lost: and driven away: even her name
Unknown. O fool, to have wasted for a kiss
Time when they could have talked! An angry shame
Was in him. He had worshipt earth, and this
—The venomed clouds fire spitting from the abyss,
This was the truth indeed, the world's intent
Unmasked and naked now, the thing it meant.

7

The storm lay on the forest a great time
—Wheeled in its thundery circuit, turned, returned.
Still through the dead-leaved darkness, through the slime

Of standing pools and slots of clay storm-churned
Went Dymer. Still the knotty lightning burned
Along black air. He heard the unbroken sound
Of water rising in the hollower ground.

8

He cursed it in his madness, flung it back,
Sorrow as wild as young men's sorrows are,
Till, after midnight, when the tempest's track
Drew off, between two clouds appeared one star.
Then his mood changed. And this was heavier far,
When bit by bit, rarer and still more rare,
The weakening thunder ceased from the cleansed air;

9

When the leaves began to drip with dying rain
And trees showed black against the glimmering sky,
When the night-birds flapped out and called again
Above him: when the silence cool and shy
Came stealing to its own, and streams ran by
Now audible amid the rustling wood
—Oh, then came the worst hour for flesh and blood.

10

It was no nightmare now with fiery stream
Too horrible to last, able to blend
Itself and all things in one hurrying dream;
It was the waking world that will not end
Because hearts break, that is not foe nor friend,
Where sane and settled knowledge first appears
Of work-day desolation, with no tears.

[38]

He halted then, footsore, weary to death,
And heard his heart beating in solitude,
When suddenly the sound of sharpest breath
Indrawn with pain and the raw smell of blood
Surprised his sense. Near by to where he stood
Came a long whimpering moan—a broken word,
A rustle of leaves where some live body stirred.

12

He groped towards the sound. 'What, brother, brother,
Who groaned?'—'I'm hit. I'm finished. Let me be.'
—'Put out your hand, then. Reach me. No, the other.'
—'Don't touch. Fool! Damn you! Leave me.'—'I can't see.
Where are you?' Then more groans. 'They've done for me.
I've no hands. Don't come near me. No, but stay,
Don't leave me . . . O my God! Is it near day?'

13

—'Soon now, a little longer. Can you sleep?
I'll watch for you.'—'Sleep, is it? That's ahead,
But none till then. Listen: I've bled too deep
To last out till the morning. I'll be dead
Within the hour—sleep then. I've heard it said
They don't mind at the last, but this is Hell.
If I'd the strength—I have such things to tell.'

14

All trembling in the dark and sweated over
Like a man reared in peace, unused to pain,
Sat Dymer near him in the lightless cover,
Afraid to touch and shamefaced to refrain.

Then bit by bit and often checked again
With agony the voice told on. (The place
Was dark, that neither saw the other's face.)

15

'There is a City which men call in scorn
The Perfect City—eastward of this wood—
You've heard about the place. There I was born.
I'm one of them, their work. Their sober mood,
The ordered life, the laws, are in my blood
—A life . . . well, less than happy, something more
Than the red greed and lusts that went before.

16

'All in one day, one man and at one blow
Brought ruin on us all. There was a boy
—Blue eyes, large limbs, were all he had to show,
You need no greater prophets to destroy.
He seemed a man asleep. Sorrow and joy
Had passed him by—the dreamiest, safest man,
The most obscure, until this curse began.

17

'Then—how or why it was, I cannot say—
This Dymer, this fool baby pink-and-white,
Went mad beneath his quiet face. One day,
With nothing said, he rose and laughed outright
Before his master: then, in all our sight,
Even where we sat to watch, he struck him dead
And screamed with laughter once again and fled.

18

'Lord! how it all comes back. How still the place is,
And he there lying dead . . . only the sound
Of a bluebottle buzzing . . . sharpened faces
Strained, gaping from the benches all around . . .
The dead man hunched and quiet with no wound,
And minute after minute terror creeping
With dreadful hopes to set the wild heart leaping.

19

'Then one by one at random (no word spoken)
We slipt out to the sunlight and away.
We felt the empty sense of something broken
And comfortless adventure all that day.
Men loitered at their work and could not say
What trembled at their lips or what new light
Was in girls' eyes. Yet we endured till night.

20

'Then . . . I was lying awake in bed,
Shot through with tremulous thought, lame hopes, and sweet
Desire of reckless days—with burning head.
And then there came a clamour from the street,
Came nearer, nearer, nearer—stamping feet
And screaming song and curses and a shout
Of "Who's for Dymer, Dymer?—Up and out!"

21

'We looked out from our window. Thronging there
A thousand of our people, girls and men,
Raved and reviled and shouted by the glare
Of torches and of bonfire blaze. And then

[41]

Came tumult from the street beyond: again
"Dymer!" they cried. And farther off there came
The sound of gun-fire and the gleam of flame.

22

'I rushed down with the rest. Oh, we were mad!
After this, it's all nightmare. The black sky
Between the housetops framed was all we had
To tell us that the old world could not die
And that we were no gods. The flood ran high
When first I came, but after was the worse,
Oh, to recall . . .! On Dymer rest the curse!

23

'Our leader was a hunchback with red hair
—Bran was his name. He had that kind of force
About him that will hold your eyes fast there
As in ten miles of green one patch of gorse
Will hold them—do you know? His lips were coarse,
But his eyes like a prophet's—seemed to fill
The whole face. And his tongue was never still.

24

'He cried: "As Dymer broke, we'll break the chain.
The world is free. They taught you to be chaste
And labour and bear orders and refrain.
Refrain? From what? All's good enough. We'll taste
Whatever is. Life murmurs from the waste
Beneath the mind . . . who made the reasoning part
The jailer of the wild gods in the heart?"

[42]

25

'We were a ragtail crew—wild-haired, half-dressed,
All shouting, "Up, for Dymer! Up away!"
Yet each one always watching all the rest
And looking to his back. And some were gay
Like drunk men, some were cringing, pinched and grey
With terror dry on the lip. (The older ones
Had had the sense enough to bring their guns.)

26

'The wave where I was swallowed swelled and broke,
After long surge, into the open square.
And here there was more light: new clamour woke.
Here first I heard the bullets sting the air
And went hot round the heart. Our lords were there
In barricade with all their loyal men.
For every one man loyal Bran led ten.

27

'Then charge and cheer and bubbling sobs of death,
We hovered on their front. Like swarming bees
Their spraying bullets came—no time for breath.
I saw men's stomachs fall out on their knees;
And shouting faces, while they shouted, freeze
Into black, bony masks. Before we knew
We're into them . . . "Swine!"—"Die, then!"—"That's for you!"

28

'The next that I remember was a lull
And sated pause. I saw an old, old man
Lying before my feet with shattered skull,
And both my arms dripped red. And then came Bran
And at his heels a hundred murderers ran,

[43]

With prisoners now, clamouring to take and try them
And burn them, wedge their nails up, crucify them.

29

'God! . . . Once the lying spirit of a cause
With maddening words dethrones the mind of men,
They're past the reach of prayer. The eternal laws
Hate them. Their eyes will not come clean again,
But doom and strong delusion drive them then
Without ruth, without rest . . . the iron laughter
Of the immortal mouths goes hooting after.

30

'And we had firebrands too. Tower after tower
Fell sheathed in thundering flame. The street was like
A furnace mouth. We had them in our power!
Then was the time to mock them and to strike,
To flay men and spit women on the pike,
Bidding them dance. Wherever the most shame
Was done the doer called on Dymer's name.

31

'Faces of men in torture . . . from my mind
They will not go away. The East lay still
In darkness when we left the town behind
Flaming to light the fields. We'd had our will:
We sang, "Oh, we will make the frost distil
From Time's grey forehead into living dew
And break whatever has been and build new."

32

'Day found us on the border of this wood,
Blear-eyed and pale. Then the most part began

To murmur and to lag, crying for food
And shelter. But we dared not answer Bran.
Wherever in the ranks the murmur ran
He'd find it—"You, there, whispering. Up, you sneak,
Reactionary, eh? Come out and speak."

33

'Then there'd be shrieks, a pistol shot, a cry,
And someone down. I was the third he caught.
The others pushed me out beneath his eye,
Saying, "He's here; here, Captain." Who'd have thought—
My old friends? But I know now. I've been taught . . .
They cut away my two hands and my feet
And laughed and left me for the birds to eat.

34

'Oh, God's name! If I had my hands again
And Dymer here . . . it would not be my blood.
I am stronger now than he is, old with pain,
One grip would make him mine. But it's no good,
I'm dying fast. Look stranger, where the wood
Grows lighter. It's the morning. Stranger dear,
Don't leave me. Talk a little while. Come near.'

35

But Dymer, sitting hunched with knee to chin,
Close to the dying man, answered no word.
His face was stone. There was no meaning in
His wakeful eyes. Sometimes the other stirred
And fretted, near his death; and Dymer heard,
Yet sat like one that neither hears nor sees.
And the cold East whitened beyond the trees.

CANTO V

1

Through bearded cliffs a valley has driven thus deep
Its wedge into the mountain and no more.
The faint track of the farthest-wandering sheep
Ends here, and the grey hollows at their core
Of silence feel the dulled continuous roar
Of higher streams. At every step the skies
Grow less and in their place black ridges rise.

2

Hither, long after noon, with plodding tread
And eyes on earth, grown dogged, Dymer came,
Who all the long day in the woods had fled
From the horror of those lips that screamed his name
And cursed him. Busy wonder and keen shame
Were driving him, and little thoughts like bees
Followed and pricked him on and left no ease.

3

Now, when he looked and saw this emptiness
Seven times enfolded in the idle hills,
There came a chilly pause to his distress,
A cloud of the deep world-despair that fills
A man's heart like the incoming tide and kills
All pains except its own. In that broad sea
No hope, no change, and no regret can be.

4

He felt the eternal strength of the silly earth,
The unhastening circuit of the stars and sea,
The business of perpetual death and birth,
The meaningless precision. All must be
The same and still the same in each degree—
Who cared now? And he smiled and could forgive,
Believing that for sure he would not live.

Then, where he saw a little water run
Beneath a bush, he slept. The chills of May
Came dropping and the stars peered one by one
Out of the deepening blue, while far away
The western brightness dulled to bars of grey.
Half-way to midnight, suddenly, from dreaming
He woke wide into present horror, screaming.

6

For he had dreamt of being in the arms
Of his beloved and in quiet places;
But all at once it filled with night alarms
And rapping guns: and men with splintered faces,
—No eyes, no nose, all red—were running races
With worms along the floor. And he ran out
To find the girl and shouted: and that shout

Had carried him into the waking world.
There stood the concave, vast, unfriendly night,
And over him the scroll of stars unfurled.
Then wailing like a child he rose upright,
Heart-sick with desolation. The new blight

Of loss had nipt him sore, and sad self-pity
Thinking of her—then thinking of the City.

8

For, in each moment's thought, the deeds of Bran,
The burning and the blood and his own shame,
Would tease him into madness till he ran
For refuge to the thought of her; whence came
Utter and endless loss—no, not a name,
Not a word, nothing left—himself alone
Crying amid that valley of old stone:

9

'How soon it all ran out! And I suppose
They, they up there, the old contriving powers,
They knew it all the time—for someone knows
And waits and watches till we pluck the flowers,
Then leaps. So soon—my store of happy hours
All gone before I knew. I have expended
My whole wealth in a day. It's finished, ended.

10

'And nothing left. Can it be possible
That joy flows through and, when the course is run,
It leaves no change, no mark on us to tell
Its passing? And as poor as we've begun
We end the richest day? What we have won,
Can it all die like this? . . . Joy flickers on
The razor-edge of the present and is gone.

11

'What have I done to bear upon my name
The curse of Bran? I was not of his crew,

Nor any man's. And Dymer has the blame—
What have I done? Wronged whom? I never knew.
What's Bran to me? I had my deed to do
And ran out by myself, alone and free.
—Why should earth sing with joy and not for me?

12

'Ah, but the earth never did sing for joy . . .
There is a glamour on the leaf and flower
And April comes and whistles to a boy
Over white fields: and, beauty has such power
Upon us, he believes her in that hour,
For who could not believe? Can it be false,
All that the blackbird says and the wind calls?

13

'What have I done? No living thing I made
Nor wished to suffer harm. I sought my good
Because the spring was gloriously arrayed
And the blue eyebright misted all the wood.
Yet to obey that springtime and my blood,
This was to be unarmed and off my guard
And gave God time to hit once and hit hard.

14

'The men built right who made that City of ours,
They knew their world. A man must crouch to face
Infinite malice, watching at all hours,
Shut Nature out—give her no moment's space
For entry. The first needs of all our race
Are walls, a den, a cover. Traitor I
Who first ran out beneath the open sky.

[49]

15

'Our fortress and fenced place I made to fall,
I slipt the sentries and let in the foe.
I have lost my brothers and my love and all.
Nothing is left but me. Now let me go.
I have seen the world stripped naked and I know.
Great God, take back your world. I will have none
Of all your glittering gauds but death alone.'

16

Meanwhile the earth swung round in hollow night.
Souls without number in all nations slept
Snug on her back, safe speeding towards the light;
Hours tolled, and in damp woods the night beast crept,
And over the long seas the watch was kept
In black ships, twinkling onward, green and red:
Always the ordered stars moved overhead.

17

And no one knew that Dymer in his scales
Had weighed all these and found them nothing worth.
Indifferently the dawn that never fails
Troubled the east of night with gradual birth,
Whispering a change of colours on cold earth,
And a bird woke, then two. The sunlight ran
Along the hills and yellow day began.

18

But stagnant gloom clung in the valley yet;
Hills crowded out a third part of the sky,
Black-looking, and the boulders dripped with wet:
No bird sang. Dymer, shivering, heaved a sigh

And yawned and said: 'It's cruel work to die
Of hunger'; and again, with cloudy breath
Blown between chattering teeth, 'It's a bad death.'

19

He crouched and clasped his hands about his knees
And hugged his own limbs for the pitiful sense
Of homeliness they had—familiars these,
This body, at least, his own, his last defence.
But soon his morning misery drove him thence,
Eating his heart, to wander as chance led
On, upward, to the narrowing gully's head.

20

The cloud lay on the nearest mountain-top
As from a giant's chimney smoking there,
But Dymer took no heed. Sometimes he'd stop,
Sometimes he hurried faster, as despair
Pricked deeper, and cried out: 'Even now, somewhere,
Bran with his crew's at work. They rack, they burn,
And there's no help in me. I've served their turn.'

21

Meanwhile the furrowed fog rolled down ahead,
Long tatters of its vanguard smearing round
The bases of the crags. Like cobweb shed
Down the deep combes it dulled the tinkling sound
Of water on the hills. The spongy ground
Faded three yards ahead: then nearer yet
Fell the cold wreaths, the white depth gleaming wet.

[51]

22

Then after a long time the path he trod
Led downward. Then all suddenly it dipped
Far steeper, and yet steeper, with smooth sod.
He was half running now. A stone that slipped
Beneath him, rattled headlong down: he tripped,
Stumbled and clutched—then panic, and no hope
To stop himself, once lost upon that slope.

23

And faster, ever faster, and his eye
Caught tree-tops far below. The nightmare feeling
Had gripped him. He was screaming: and the sky
Seemed hanging upside down. Then struggling, reeling,
With effort beyond thought he hung half kneeling,
Halted one saving moment. With wild will
He clawed into the hillside and lay still,

24

Half hanging on both arms. His idle feet
Dangled and found no hold. The moor lay wet
Against him and he sweated with the heat
Of terror, all alive. His teeth were set.
'By God, I will not die,' said he; 'not yet.'
Then slowly, slowly, with enormous strain,
He heaved himself an inch: then heaved again,

25

Till saved and spent he lay. He felt indeed
It was the big, round world beneath his breast,
The mother planet proven at his need.
The shame of glad surrender stood confessed,
He cared not for his boasts. This, this was best,
This giving up of all. He need not strive;
He panted, he lay still, he was alive.

And now his eyes were closed. Perhaps he slept,
Lapt in unearthly quiet—never knew
How bit by bit the fog's white rearguard crept
Over the crest and faded, and the blue
First brightening at the zenith trembled through,
And deepening shadows took a sharper form
Each moment, and the sandy earth grew warm.

27

Yet, dreaming of blue skies, in dream he heard
The pure voice of a lark that seemed to send
Its song from heights beyond all height. That bird
Sang out of heaven, 'The world will never end,'
Sang from the gates of heaven, 'Will never end.'
Sang till it seemed there was no other thing
But bright space and one voice set there to sing.

28

It seemed to be the murmur and the voice
Of beings beyond number, each and all
Singing I AM. Each of itself made choice
And was: whence flows the justice that men call
Divine. She keeps the great worlds lest they fall
From hour to hour, and makes the hills renew
Their ancient youth and sweetens all things through.

29

It seemed to be the low voice of the world
Brooding alone beneath the strength of things,
Murmuring of days and nights and years unfurled
Forever, and the unwearied joy that brings
Out of old fields the flowers of unborn springs,
Out of old wars and cities burned with wrong,
A splendour in the dark, a tale, a song.

[53]

30

The dream ran thin towards waking, and he knew
It was but a bird's piping with no sense.
He rolled round on his back. The sudden blue,
Quivering with light, hard, cloudless and intense,
Shone over him. The lark still sounded thence
And stirred him at the heart. Some spacious thought
Was passing by too gently to be caught.

31

With that he thrust the damp hair from his face
And sat upright. The perilous cliff dropped sheer
Before him, close at hand, and from his place
Listening in mountain silence he could hear
Birds crying far below. It was not fear
That took him, but strange glory, when his eye
Looked past the edge into surrounding sky.

32

He rose and stood. Then lo! the world beneath
—Wide pools that in the sun-splashed foothills lay,
Sheep-dotted downs, soft-piled, and rolling heath,
River and shining weir and steeples grey
And the green waves of forest. Far away
Distance rose heaped on distance: nearer hand,
The white roads leading down to a new land.

CANTO VI

I

The sun was high in heaven and Dymer stood
A bright speck on the endless mountain-side,
Till, blossom after blossom, that rich mood
Faded and truth rolled homeward, like a tide
Before whose edge the weak soul fled to hide
In vain, with ostrich head, through many a shape
Of coward fancy, whimpering for escape.

2

But only for a moment; then his soul
Took the full swell and heaved a dripping prow
Clear of the shattering wave-crest. He was whole.
No veils should hide the truth, no truth should cow
The dear self-pitying heart. 'I'll babble now
No longer,' Dymer said. 'I'm broken in.
Pack up the dreams and let the life begin.'

3

With this he turned. 'I must have food to-day,'
He muttered. Then among the cloudless hills
By winding tracks he sought the downward way
And followed the steep course of tumbling rills
—Came to the glens the wakening mountain fills
In springtime with the echoing splash and shock
Of waters leaping cold from rock to rock.

[55]

4

And still, it seemed, that lark with its refrain
Sang in the sky, and wind was in his hair
And hope at heart. Then once, and once again,
He heard a gun fired off. It broke the air
As a stone breaks a pond, and everywhere
The dry crags echoed clear: and at the sound
Once a big bird rose whirring from the ground.

In half an hour he reached the level land
And followed the field-paths and crossed the stiles,
Then looked and saw, near by, on his left hand
An old house, folded round with billowy piles
Of dark yew hedge. The moss was on the tiles,
The pigeons in the yard, and in the tower
A clock that had no hands and told no hour.

6

He hastened. In warm waves the garden scent
Came stronger at each stride. The mountain breeze
Was gone. He reached the gates; then in he went
And seemed to lose the sky—such weight of trees
Hung overhead. He heard the noise of bees
And saw, far off, in the blue shade between
The windless elms, one walking on the green.

It was a mighty man whose beardless face
Beneath grey hair shone out so large and mild
It made a sort of moonlight in the place.
A dreamy desperation, wistful-wild,

[56]

Showed in his glance and gait: yet like a child,
An Asian emperor's only child, was he
With his grave looks and bright solemnity.

8

And over him there hung the witching air,
The wilful courtesy, of the days of old,
The graces wherein idleness grows fair;
And somewhat in his sauntering walk he rolled
And toyed about his waist with seals of gold,
Or stood to ponder often in mid-stride,
Tilting his heavy head upon one side.

9

When Dymer had called twice, he turned his eye:
Then, coming out of silence (as a star
All in one moment slips into the sky
Of evening, yet we feel it comes from far),
He said, 'Sir, you are welcome. Few there are
That come my way': and in huge hands he pressed
Dymer's cold hand and bade him in to rest.

10

'How did you find this place out? Have you heard
My gun? It was but now I killed a lark.'
'What, Sir!' said Dymer; 'shoot the singing bird?'
'Sir,' said the man, 'they sing from dawn till dark,
And interrupt my dreams too long. But hark ...
Another? Did you hear no singing? No?
It was my fancy, then ... pray, let it go.

11

'From here you see my garden's only flaw.
Stand here, Sir, at the dial.' Dymer stood.

The Master pointed; then he looked and saw
How hedges and the funeral quietude
Of black trees fringed the garden like a wood,
And only, in one place, one gap that showed
The blue side of the hills, the white hill-road.

12

'I have planted fir and larch to fill the gap,'
He said, 'because this too makes war upon
The art of dream. But by some great mishap
Nothing I plant will grow there. We pass on ...
The sunshine of the afternoon is gone.
Let us go in. It draws near time to sup
—I hate the garden till the moon is up.'

13

They passed from the hot lawn into the gloom
And coolness of the porch: then, past a door
That opened with no noise, into a room
Where green leaves choked the window and the floor
Sank lower than the ground. A tattered store
Of brown books met the eye: a crystal ball:
And masks with empty eyes along the wall.

14

Then Dymer sat, but knew not how nor where,
And supper was set out before these two,
—He saw not how—with silver old and rare
But tarnished. And he ate and never knew
What meats they were. At every bite he grew
More drowsy and let slide his crumbling will.
The Master at his side was talking still.

15

And all his talk was tales of magic words
And of the nations in the clouds above,
Astral and aerish tribes who fish for birds
With angles. And by history he could prove
How chosen spirits from earth had won their love,
As Arthur, or Usheen: and to their isle
Went Helen for the sake of a Greek smile.

And ever in his talk he mustered well
His texts and strewed old authors round the way,
'Thus Wierus writes,' and 'Thus the Hermetics tell,'
'This was Agrippa's view,' and 'Others say
With Cardan,' till he had stolen quite away
Dymer's dull wits and softly drawn apart
The ivory gates of hope that change the heart.

17

Dymer was talking now. Now Dymer told
Of his own love and losing, drowsily.
The Master leaned towards him, 'Was it cold,
This spirit, to the touch?'—'No, Sir, not she,'
Said Dymer. And his host: 'Why this must be
Aethereal, not aerial! O my soul,
Be still . . . but wait. Tell on, Sir, tell the whole.'

Then Dymer told him of the beldam too,
The old, old, matriarchal dreadfulness.
Over the Master's face a shadow drew,
He shifted in his chair and 'Yes' and 'Yes,'
He murmured twice. 'I never looked for less!
Always the same . . . that frightful woman shape
Besets the dream-way and the soul's escape.'

But now when Dymer made to talk of Bran,
A huge indifference fell upon his host,
Patient and wandering-eyed. Then he began,
'Forgive me. You are young. What helps us most
Is to find out again that heavenly ghost
Who loves you. For she was a ghost, and you
In that place where you met were ghostly too.

20

'Listen! for I can launch you on the stream
Will roll you to the shores of her own land . . .
I could be sworn you never learned to dream,
But every night you take with careless hand
What chance may bring? I'll teach you to command
The comings and the goings of your spirit
Through all that borderland which dreams inherit.

21

'You shall have hauntings suddenly. And often,
When you forget, when least you think of her
(For so you shall forget), a light will soften
Over the evening woods. And in the stir
Of morning dreams (oh, I will teach you, Sir)
There'll come a sound of wings. Or you shall be
Waked in the midnight murmuring, "It was she." '

22

'No, no,' said Dymer, 'not that way. I seem
To have slept for twenty years. Now—while I shake
Out of my eyes that dust of burdening dream,
Now when the long clouds tremble ripe to break
And the far hills appear, when first I wake,

Still blinking, struggling towards the world of men,
And longing—would you turn me back again?

23

'Dreams? I have had my dream too long. I thought
The sun rose for my sake. I ran down blind
And dancing to the abyss. Oh, Sir, I brought
Boy-laughter for a gift to gods who find
The martyr's soul too soft. But that's behind.
I'm waking now. They broke me. All ends thus
Always—and we're for them, not they for us.

24

'And she—she was no dream. It would be waste
To seek her there, the living in that den
Of lies.' The Master smiled. 'You are in haste!
For broken dreams the cure is, Dream again
And deeper. If the waking world, and men,
And nature marred your dream—so much the worse
For a crude world beneath its primal curse.'

25

—'Ah, but you do not know! Can dreams do this,
Pluck out blood-guiltiness upon the shore
Of memory—and undo what's done amiss,
And bid the thing that has been be no more?'
—'Sir, it is only dreams unlock that door,'
He answered with a shrug. 'What would you have?
In dreams the thrice-proved coward can feel brave.

26

'In dreams the fool is free from scorning voices.
Grey-headed whores are virgin there again.

Out of the past dream brings long-buried choices,
All in a moment snaps the tenfold chain
That life took years in forging. There the stain
Of oldest sins—how do the good words go?—
Though they were scarlet, shall be white as snow.'

27

Then, drawing near, when Dymer did not speak,
'My little son,' said he, 'your wrong and right
Are also dreams: fetters to bind the weak
Faster to phantom earth and blear the sight.
Wake into dreams, into the larger light
That quenches these frail stars. They will not know
Earth's bye-laws in the land to which you go.'

28

—'I must undo my sins.'—'An earthly law,
And, even in earth, the child of yesterday.
Throw down your human pity; cast your awe
Behind you; put repentance all away.
Home to the elder depths! for never they
Supped with the stars who dared not slough behind
The last shred of earth's holies from their mind.'

29

'Sir,' answered Dymer, 'I would be content
To drudge in earth, easing my heart's disgrace,
Counting a year's long service lightly spent
If once at the year's end I saw her face
Somewhere, being then most weary, in some place
I looked not for that joy—or heard her near
Whispering, "Yet courage, friend," for one more year.'

'Pish,' said the Master. 'Will you have the truth?
You think that virtue saves? Her people care
For the high heart and idle hours of youth;
For these they will descend our lower air,
Not virtue. You would nerve your arm and bear
Your burden among men? Look to it, child:
By virtue's self vision can be defiled.

31

'You will grow full of pity and the love of men,
And toil until the morning moisture dries
Out of your heart. Then once, or once again,
It may be you will find her: but your eyes
Soon will be grown too dim. The task that lies
Next to your hand will hide her. You shall be
The child of earth and gods you shall not see.'

32

Here suddenly he ceased. Tip-toes he went.
A bolt clicked—then the window creaked ajar,
And out of the wet world the hedgerow scent
Came floating; and the dark without one star
Nor shape of trees nor sense of near and far,
The undimensioned night and formless skies
Were there, and were the Master's great allies.

33

'I am very old,' he said. 'But if the time
We suffer in our dreams were counted age,
I have outlived the ocean and my prime
Is with me to this day. Years cannot gauge

The dream-life. In the turning of a page,
Dozing above my book, I have lived through
More ages than the lost Lemuria knew.

34

'I am not mortal. Were I doomed to die
This hour, in this half-hour I interpose
A thousand years of dream: and, those gone by,
As many more, and in the last of those,
Ten thousand—ever journeying towards a close
That I shall never reach: for time shall flow,
Wheel within wheel, interminably slow.

35

'And you will drink my cup and go your way
Into the valley of dreams. You have heard the call.
Come hither and escape. Why should you stay?
Earth is a sinking ship, a house whose wall
Is tottering while you sweep; the roof will fall
Before the work is done. You cannot mend it.
Patch as you will, at last the rot must end it.'

36

Then Dymer lifted up his heavy head
Like Atlas on broad shoulders bearing up
The insufferable globe. 'I had not said,'
He mumbled, 'never said I'd taste the cup.
What, is it this you give me? Must I sup?
Oh, lies, all lies . . . Why did you kill the lark?
Guide me the cup to lip . . . it is so dark.'

CANTO VII

1

The host had trimmed his lamp. The downy moth
Came from the garden. Where the lamplight shed
Its circle of smooth white upon the cloth,
Down mid the rinds of fruit and broken bread,
Upon his sprawling arms lay Dymer's head;
And often, as he dreamed, he shifted place,
Muttering and showing half his drunken face.

2

The beating stillness of the dead of night
Flooded the room. The dark and sleepy powers
Settled upon the house and filled it quite;
Far from the roads it lay, from belfry towers
And hen-roosts, in a world of folded flowers,
Buried in loneliest fields where beasts that love
The silence through the unrustled hedgerows move.

3

Now from the Master's lips there breathed a sigh
As of a man released from some control
That wronged him. Without aim his wandering eye,
Unsteadied and unfixed, began to roll.
His lower lip dropped loose. The informing soul
Seemed fading from his face. He laughed out loud
Once only: then looked round him, hushed and cowed.

[65]

4

Then, summoning all himself, with tightened lip,
With desperate coolness and attentive air,
He touched between his thumb and finger-tip,
Each in its turn, the four legs of his chair,
Then back again in haste—there!—that one there
Had been forgotten . . . once more! . . . safer now;
That's better! and he smiled and cleared his brow.

5

Yet this was but a moment's ease. Once more
He glanced about him like a startled hare,
His big eyes bulged with horror. As before,
Quick!—to the touch that saves him. But despair
Is nearer by one step; and in his chair
Huddling he waits. He knows that they'll come strong
Again and yet again and all night long;

6

And after this night comes another night
—Night after night until the worst of all.
And now too even the noonday and the light
Let through the horrors. Oh, could he recall
The deep sleep and the dreams that used to fall
Around him for the asking! But, somehow,
Something's amiss . . . sleep comes so rarely now.

7

Then, like the dog returning to its vomit,
He staggered to the bookcase to renew
Yet once again the taint he had taken from it,
And shuddered as he went. But horror drew
His feet, as joy draws others. There in view
Was his strange heaven and his far stranger hell,
His secret lust, his soul's dark citadel:—

8

Old Theomagia, Demonology,
Cabbala, Chemic Magic, Book of the Dead,
Damning Hermetic rolls that none may see
Save the already damned—such grubs are bred
From minds that lose the Spirit and seek instead
For spirits in the dust of dead men's error,
Buying the joys of dream with dreamland terror.

9

This lost soul looked them over one and all,
Now sickening at the heart's root; for he knew
This night was one of those when he would fall
And scream alone (such things they made him do)
And roll upon the floor. The madness grew
Wild at his breast, but still his brain was clear
That he could watch the moment coming near.

10

But, ere it came, he heard a sound, half groan,
Half muttering, from the table. Like a child
Caught unawares that thought it was alone,
He started as in guilt. His gaze was wild,
Yet pitiably with all his will he smiled,
—So strong is shame, even then. And Dymer stirred,
Now waking, and looked up and spoke one word:

11

'Water!' he said. He was too dazed to see
What hell-wrung face looked down, what shaking hand
Poured out the draught. He drank it thirstily
And held the glass for more. 'Your land . . . your land
Of dreams,' he said. 'All lies! . . . I understand
More than I did. Yes, water. I've the thirst
Of hell itself. Your magic's all accursed.'

12

When he had drunk again he rose and stood,
Pallid and cold with sleep. 'By God,' he said,
'You did me wrong to send me to that wood.
I sought a living spirit and found instead
Bogies and wraiths.' The Master raised his head,
Calm as a sage, and answered, 'Are you mad?
Come, sit you down. Tell me what dream you had.'

13

—'I dreamed about a wood . . . an autumn red
Of beech-trees big as mountains. Down between—
The first thing that I saw—a clearing spread,
Deep down, oh, very deep. Like some ravine
Or like a well it sank, that forest green
Under its weight of forest—more remote
Than one ship in a landlocked sea afloat.

14

'Then through the narrowed sky some heavy bird
Would flap its way, a stillness more profound
Following its languid wings. Sometimes I heard
Far off in the long woods with quiet sound
The sudden chestnut thumping to the ground,
Or the dry leaf that drifted past upon
Its endless loiter earthward and was gone.

15

'Then next . . . I heard twigs splintering on my right
And rustling in the thickets. Turning there
I watched. Out of the foliage came in sight
The head and blundering shoulders of a bear,

Glistening in sable black, with beady stare
Of eyes towards me, and no room to fly
—But padding soft and slow the beast came by.

16

'And—mark their flattery—stood and rubbed his flank
Against me. On my shaken legs I felt
His heart beat. And my hand that stroked him sank
Wrist-deep upon his shoulder in soft pelt.
Yes . . . and across my spirit as I smelt
The wild thing's scent, a new, sweet wildness ran
Whispering of Eden-fields long lost by man.

17

'So far was well. But then came emerald birds
Singing about my head. I took my way
Sauntering the cloistered woods. Then came the herds,
The roebuck and the fallow deer at play,
Trooping to nose my hand. All this, you say,
Was sweet? Oh, sweet! . . . do you think I could not see
That beasts and wood were nothing else but me?

18

'. . . That I was making everything I saw,
Too sweet, far too well fitted to desire
To be a living thing? Those forests draw
No sap from the kind earth: the solar fire
And soft rain feed them not: that fairy brier
Pricks not: the birds sing sweetly in that brake
Not for their own delight but for my sake!

19

'It is a world of sad, cold, heartless stuff,
Like a bought smile, no joy in it.'—'But stay;
Did you not find your lady?'—'Sure enough!
I still had hopes till then. The autumn day
Was westering, the long shadows crossed my way,
When over daisies folded for the night
Beneath rook-gathering elms she came in sight.'

20

—'Was she not fair?'—'So beautiful, she seemed
Almost a living soul. But every part
Was what I made it—all that I had dreamed—
No more, no less: the mirror of my heart,
Such things as boyhood feigns beneath the smart
Of solitude and spring. I was deceived
Almost. In that first moment I believed.

21

'For a big, brooding rapture, tense as fire
And calm as a first sleep, had soaked me through
Without thought, without word, without desire . . .
Meanwhile above our heads the deepening blue
Burnished the gathering stars. Her sweetness drew
A veil before my eyes. The minutes passed
Heavy like loaded vines. She spoke at last.

22

'She said, for this land only did men love
The shadow-lands of earth. All our disease
Of longing, all the hopes we fabled of,

[70]

Fortunate islands or Hesperian seas
Or woods beyond the West, were but the breeze
That blew from off those shores: one far, spent breath
That reached even to the world of change and death.

23

'She told me I had journeyed home at last
Into the golden age and the good countrie
That had been always there. She bade me cast
My cares behind forever:—on her knee
Worshipped me, lord and love—oh, I can see
Her red lips even now! Is it not wrong
That men's delusions should be made so strong?

24

'For listen, I was so besotted now
She made me think that I was somehow seeing
The very core of truth ... I felt somehow,
Beyond all veils, the inward pulse of being.
Thought was enslaved, but oh, it felt like freeing
And draughts of larger air. It is too much!
Who can come through untainted from that touch?

25

'There I was nearly wrecked. But mark the rest:
She went too fast. Soft to my arms she came.
The robe slipped from her shoulder. The smooth breast
Was bare against my own. She shone like flame
Before me in the dusk, all love, all shame—
Faugh!—and it was myself. But all was well,
For, at the least, that moment snapped the spell.

26

'As when you light a candle, the great gloom
Which was the unbounded night, sinks down, compressed
To four white walls in one familiar room,
So the vague joy shrank wilted in my breast
And narrowed to one point, unmasked, confessed;
Fool's paradise was gone: instead was there
King Lust with his black, sudden, serious stare.

27

'That moment in a cloud among the trees
Wild music and the glare of torches came.
On sweated faces, on the prancing knees
Of shaggy satyrs fell the smoky flame,
On ape and goat and crawlers without name,
On rolling breast, black eyes and tossing hair,
On old bald-headed witches, lean and bare.

28

'They beat the devilish tom-tom rub-a-dub;
Lunging, leaping, in unwieldy romp,
Singing Cotytto and Beelzebub,
With devil-dancers' mask and phallic pomp,
Torn raw with briers and caked from many a swamp,
They came, among the wild flowers dripping blood
And churning the green mosses into mud.

29

'They sang, "Return! Return! We are the lust
That was before the world and still shall be
When your last law is trampled into dust,
We are the mother swamp, the primal sea

Whence the dry land appeared. Old, old are we.
It is but a return . . . it's nothing new,
Easy as slipping on a well-worn shoe."

30

'And then there came warm mouths and finger-tips
Preying upon me, whence I could not see,
Then . . . a huge face, low-browed, with swollen lips
Crooning, "I am not beautiful as she,
But I'm the older love; you shall love me
Far more than Beauty's self. You have been ours
Always. We are the world's most ancient powers."

31

'First flatterer and then bogy—like a dream!
Sir, are you listening? Do you also know
How close to the soft laughter comes the scream
Down yonder?' But his host cried sharply, 'No.
Leave me alone. Why will you plague me? Go!
Out of my house! Begone!'—'With all my heart,'
Said Dymer. 'But one word before we part.'

32

He paused, and in his cheek the anger burned:
Then turning to the table, he poured out
More water. But before he drank he turned—
Then leaped back to the window with a shout
For there—it was no dream—beyond all doubt
He saw the Master crouch with levelled gun,
Cackling in maniac voice, 'Run, Dymer, run!'

33

He ducked and sprang far out. The starless night
On the wet lawn closed round him every way.
Then came the gun-crack and the splash of light
Vanished as soon as seen. Cool garden clay
Slid from his feet. He had fallen and he lay
Face downward among leaves—then up and on
Through branch and leaf till sense and breath were gone.

CANTO VIII

1

When next he found himself no house was there,
No garden and great trees. Beside a lane
In grass he lay. Now first he was aware
That, all one side, his body glowed with pain:
And the next moment and the next again
Was neither less nor more. Without a pause
It clung like a great beast with fastened claws;

2

That for a time he could not frame a thought
Nor know himself for self, nor pain for pain,
Till moment added on to moment taught
The new, strange art of living on that plane,
Taught how the grappled soul must still remain,
Still choose and think and understand beneath
The very grinding of the ogre's teeth.

3

He heard the wind along the hedges sweep,
The quarter striking from a neighbouring tower.
About him was the weight of the world's sleep;
Within, the thundering pain. That quiet hour
Heeded it not. It throbbed, it raged with power
Fit to convulse the heavens: and at his side
The soft peace drenched the meadows far and wide.

[75]

4

The air was cold, the earth was cold with dew,
The hedge behind him dark as ink. But now
The clouds broke and a paler heaven showed through
Spacious with sudden stars, breathing somehow
The sense of change to slumbering lands. A cow
Coughed in the fields behind. The puddles showed
Like pools of sky amid the darker road.

5

And he could see his own limbs faintly white
And the blood black upon them. Then by chance
He turned . . . and it was strange: there at his right
He saw a woman standing, and her glance
Met his: and at the meeting his deep trance
Changed not, and while he looked the knowledge grew
She was not of the old life but the new.

6

'Who is it?' he said. 'The loved one, the long lost.'
He stared upon her. 'Truly?'—'Truly indeed.'
—'Oh, lady, you come late. I am tempest-tossed,
Broken and wrecked. I am dying. Look, I bleed.
Why have you left me thus and given no heed
To all my prayers?—left me to be the game
Of all deceits?'—'You should have asked my name.'

7

—'What are you, then?' But to his sudden cry
She did not answer. When he had thought awhile
He said: 'How can I tell it is no lie?
It may be one more phantom to beguile

[76]

The brain-sick dreamer with its harlot smile.'
'I have not smiled,' she said. The neighbouring bell
Tolled out another quarter. Silence fell.

8

And after a long pause he spoke again:
'Leave me,' he said. 'Why do you watch with me?
You do not love me. Human tears and pain
And hoping for the things that cannot be,
And blundering in the night where none can see,
And courage with cold back against the wall,
You do not understand.'—'I know them all.

9

'The gods themselves know pain, the eternal forms.
In realms beyond the reach of cloud, and skies
Nearest the ends of air, where come no storms
Nor sound of earth, I have looked into their eyes
Peaceful and filled with pain beyond surmise,
Filled with an ancient woe man cannot reach
One moment though in fire; yet calm their speech.'

10

'Then these,' said Dymer, 'were the world I wooed . . .
These were the holiness of flowers and grass
And desolate dews . . . these, the eternal mood
Blowing the eternal theme through men that pass.
I called myself their lover—I that was
Less fit for that long service than the least
Dull, workday drudge of men or faithful beast.

11

'Why do they lure to them such spirits as mine,
The weak, the passionate, and the fool of dreams?

When better men go safe and never pine
With whisperings at the heart, soul-sickening gleams
Of infinite desire, and joy that seems
The promise of full power? For it was they,
The gods themselves, that led me on this way.

12

'Give me the truth! I ask not now for pity.
When gods call, can the following them be sin?
Was it false light that lured me from the City?
Where was the path—without it or within?
Must it be one blind throw to lose or win?
Has heaven no voice to help? Must things of dust
Guess their own way in the dark?' She said, 'They must.'

13

Another silence: then he cried in wrath,
'You came in human shape, in sweet disguise
Wooing me, lurking for me in my path,
Hid your eternal cold with woman's eyes,
Snared me with shows of love—and all was lies.'
She answered, 'For our kind must come to all
If bidden, but in the shape for which they call.'

14

'What!' answered Dymer. 'Do you change and sway
To serve us, as the obedient planets spin
About the sun? Are you but potter's clay
For us to mould—unholy to our sin
And holy to the holiness within?'
She said, 'Waves fall on many an unclean shore,
Yet the salt seas are holy as before.

[78]

'Our nature is no purer for the saint
That worships, nor from him that uses ill
Our beauty can we suffer any taint.
As from the first we were, so are we still:
With incorruptibles the mortal will
Corrupts itself, and clouded eyes will make
Darkness within from beams they cannot take.'

'Well . . . it is well,' said Dymer. 'If I have used
The embreathing spirit amiss . . . what would have been
The strength of all my days I have refused
And plucked the stalk, too hasty, in the green,
Trusted the good for best, and having seen
Half-beauty, or beauty's fringe, the lowest stair,
The common incantation, worshipped there.'

But presently he cried in his great pain,
'If I had loved a beast it would repay,
But I have loved the Spirit and loved in vain.
Now let me die . . . ah, but before the way
Is ended quite, in the last hour of day,
Is there no word of comfort, no one kiss
Of human love? Does it all end in this?'

She answered, 'Never ask of life and death.
Uttering these names you dream of wormy clay
Or of surviving ghosts. This withering breath
Of words is the beginning of decay
In truth, when truth grows cold and pines away
Among the ancestral images. Your eyes
First see her dead: and more, the more she dies.

'You are still dreaming, dreams you shall forget
When you have cast your fetters, far from here.
Go forth; the journey is not ended yet.
You have seen Dymer dead and on the bier
More often than you dream and dropped no tear,
You have slain him every hour. Think not at all
Of death lest into death by thought you fall.'

20

He turned to question her, then looked again,
And lo! the shape was gone. The darkness lay
Heavy as yet and a cold, shifting rain
Fell with the breeze that springs before the day.
It was an hour death loves. Across the way
The clock struck once again. He saw near by
The black shape of the tower against the sky.

21

Meanwhile above the torture and the riot
Of leaping pulse and nerve that shot with pain,
Somewhere aloof and poised in spectral quiet
His soul was thinking on. The dizzied brain
Scarce seemed her organ: link by link the chain
That bound him to the flesh was loosening fast
And the new life breathed in unmoved and vast.

22

'It was like this,' he thought—'like this, or worse,
For him that I found bleeding in the wood . . .
Blessings upon him . . . there I learned the curse
That rests on Dymer's name, and truth was good.

[80]

He has forgotten now the fire and blood,
He has forgotten that there was a man
Called Dymer. He knows not himself nor Bran.

23

'How long have I been moved at heart in vain
About this Dymer, thinking this was I . . .
Why did I follow close his joy and pain
More than another man's? For he will die,
The little cloud will vanish and the sky
Reign as before. The stars remain and earth
And Man, as in the years before my birth.

24

'There was a Dymer once who worked and played
About the City; I sloughed him off and ran.
There was a Dymer in the forest glade
Ranting alone, skulking the fates of man.
I cast him also, and a third began
And he too died. But I am none of those.
Is there another still to die . . . Who knows?'

25

Then in his pain, half wondering what he did,
He made to struggle towards that belfried place.
And groaning down the sodden bank he slid,
And groaning in the lane he left his trace
Of bloodied mire: then halted with his face
Upwards, towards the gateway, breathing hard
—An old lych-gate before a burial-yard.

26

He looked within. Between the huddling crosses,
Over the slanted tombs and sunken slate

Spread the deep quiet grass and humble mosses,
A green and growing darkness, drenched of late,
Smelling of earth and damp. He reached the gate
With failing hand. 'I will rest here,' he said,
'And the long grass will cool my burning head.'

CANTO IX

I

Even as he heard the wicket clash behind
Came a great wind beneath that seemed to tear
The solid graves apart; and deaf and blind
Whirled him upright, like smoke, through towering air
Whose levels were as steps of a sky stair.
The parching cold roughened his throat with thirst
And pricked him at the heart. This was the first.

2

And as he soared into the next degree,
Suddenly all round him he could hear
Sad strings that fretted inconsolably
And ominous horns that blew both far and near.
There broke his human heart, and his last tear
Froze scalding on his chin. But while he heard
He shot like a sped dart into the third.

3

And its first stroke of silence could destroy
The spring of tears forever and compress
From off his lips the curved bow of the boy
Forever. The sidereal loneliness
Received him, where no journeying leaves the less
Still to be journeyed through: but everywhere,
Fast though you fly, the centre still is there.

And here the well-worn fabric of our life
Fell from him. Hope and purpose were cut short,
—Even the blind trust that reaches in mid-strife
Towards some heart of things. Here blew the mort
For the world spirit herself. The last support
Was fallen away—Himself, one spark of soul,
Swam in unbroken void. He was the whole,

5

And wailing: 'Why hast Thou forsaken me?
Was there no world at all, but only I
Dreaming of gods and men?' Then suddenly
He felt the wind no more: he seemed to fly
Faster than light but free, and scaled the sky
In his own strength—as if a falling stone
Should wake to find the world's will was its own.

6

And on the instant, straight before his eyes
He looked and saw a sentry shape that stood
Leaning upon its spear, with hurrying skies
Behind it and a moonset red as blood.
Upon its head were helmet and mailed hood,
And shield upon its arm and sword at thigh,
All black and pointed sharp against the sky.

7

Then came the clink of metal, the dry sound
Of steel on rock and challenge: 'Who comes here?'
And as he heard it, Dymer at one bound
Stood in the stranger's shadow, with the spear
Between them. And his human face came near
That larger face. 'What watch is this you keep,'
Said Dymer, 'on edge of such a deep?'

8

And answer came, 'I watch both night and day
This frontier . . . there are beasts of the upper air
As beasts of the deep sea . . . one walks this way
Night after night, far scouring from his lair,
Chewing the cud of lusts which are despair
And fill not, while his mouth gapes dry for bliss
That never was.'—'What kind of beast is this?'

'A kind of things escaped that have no home,
Hunters of men. They love the spring uncurled,
The will worn down, the wearied hour. They come
At night-time when the mask is off the world
And the soul's gate ill-locked and the flag furled
—Then, softly, a pale swarm, and in disguise,
Flit past the drowsy watchman, small as flies.'

10

—'I'll see this aerish beast whereof you speak.
I'll share the watch with you.'—'Nay, little One,
Begone. You are of earth. The flesh is weak . . .'
—'What is the flesh to me? My course is run,
All but some deed still waiting to be done,
Some moment I may rise on, as the boat
Lifts with the lifting tide and steals afloat.

'You are a spirit, and it is well with you,
But I am come out of great folly and shame,
The sack of cities, wrongs I must undo . . .
But tell me of the beast, and whence it came;
Who were its sire and dam? What is its name?'
—'It is my kin. All monsters are the brood
Of heaven and earth, and mixed with holy blood.'

—'How can this be?'—'My son, sit here awhile.
There is a lady in that primal place
Where I was born, who with her ancient smile
Made glad the sons of heaven. She loved to chase
The springtime round the world. To all your race
She was a sudden quivering in the wood
Or a new thought springing in solitude.

13

'Till, in prodigious hour, one swollen with youth,
Blind from new-broken prison, knowing not
Himself nor her, nor how to mate with truth,
Lay with her in a strange and secret spot,
Mortal with her immortal, and begot
This walker-in-the-night.'—'But did you know
This mortal's name?'—'Why . . . it was long ago.

14

'And yet, I think, I bear the name in mind;
It was some famished boy whom tampering men
Had crippled in their chains and made him blind
Till their weak hour discovered them: and then
He broke that prison. Softly!—it comes again,
I have it. It was Dymer, little One,
Dymer's the name. This spectre is his son.'

15

Then, after silence, came an answering shout
From Dymer, glad and full: 'Break off! Dismiss!
Your watch is ended and your lamp is out.
Unarm, unarm. Return into your bliss.
You are relieved, Sir. I must deal with this
As in my right. For either I must slay
This beast or else be slain before the day.'

16

'So mortal and so brave?' that other said,
Smiling, and turned and looked in Dymer's eyes,
Scanning him over twice from heel to head
—Like an old sergeant's glance, grown battle-wise
To know the points of men. At last, 'Arise,'
He said, 'and wear my arms. I can withhold
Nothing; for such an hour has been foretold.'

17

Thereat, with lips as cold as the sea-surge,
He kissed the youth, and bending on one knee
Put all his armour off and let emerge
Angelic shoulders marbled gloriously
And feet like frozen speed and, plain to see,
On his wide breast dark wounds and ancient scars,
The battle honours of celestial wars.

18

Then like a squire or brother born he dressed
The young man in those plates, that dripped with cold
Upon the inside, trickling over breast
And shoulder: but without, the figured gold
Gave to the tinkling ice its jagged hold,
And the icy spear froze fast to Dymer's hand.
But where the other had stood he took his stand

19

And searched the cloudy landscape. He could see
Dim shapes like hills appearing, but the moon
Had sunk behind their backs. 'When will it be?'
Said Dymer: and the other, 'Soon now, soon.
For either he comes past us at night's noon
Or else between the night and the full day,
And down there, on your left, will be his way.'

20

—'Swear that you will not come between us two
Nor help me by a hair's weight if I bow.'
—'If you are he, if prophecies speak true,
Not heaven and all the gods can help you now.
This much I have been told, but know not how
The fight will end. Who knows? I cannot tell.'
'Sir, be content,' said Dymer. 'I know well.'

Thus Dymer stood to arms, with eyes that ranged
Through aching darkness: stared upon it, so
That all things, as he looked upon them, changed
And were not as at first. But grave and slow
The larger shade went sauntering to and fro,
Humming at first the snatches of some tune
That soldiers sing, but falling silent soon.

22

Then came steps of dawn. And though they heard
No milking cry in the fields, and no cock crew,
And out of empty air no twittering bird
Sounded from neighbouring hedges, yet they knew.
Eastward the hollow blackness paled to blue,
Then blue to white: and in the West the rare,
Surviving stars blinked feebler in cold air.

For beneath Dymer's feet the sad half-light
Discovering the new landscape oddly came,
And forms grown half familiar in the night
Looked strange again: no distance seemed the same.
And now he could see clear and call by name
Valleys and hills and woods. The phantoms all
Took shape, and made a world, at morning's call.

It was a ruinous land. The ragged stumps
Of broken trees rose out of endless clay
Naked of flower and grass: the slobbered humps
Dividing the dead pools. Against the grey
A shattered village gaped. But now the day
Was very near them and the night was past,
And Dymer understood and spoke at last.

'Now I have wooed and won you, bridal earth,
Beautiful world that lives, desire of men.
All that the spirit intended at my birth
This day shall be born into deed . . . and then
The hard day's labour comes no more again
Forever. The pain dies. The longings cease.
The ship glides under the green arch of peace.

26

'Now drink me as the sun drinks up the mist.
This is the hour to cease in, at full flood,
That asks no gift from following years—but, hist!
Look yonder! At the corner of that wood—
Look! Look there where he comes! It shocks the blood,
The first sight, eh? Now, sentinel, stand clear
And save yourself. For God's sake come not near.'

His full-grown spirit had moved without command
Or spur of the will. Before he knew, he found
That he was leaping forward spear in hand
To where that ashen brute wheeled slowly round
Nosing, and set its ears towards the sound,
The pale and heavy brute, rough-ridged behind,
And full of eyes, clinking in scaly rind.

And now ten paces parted them: and here
He halted. He thrust forward his left foot,
Poising his straightened arms, and launched the spear,
And gloriously it sang. But now the brute
Lurched forward: and he saw the weapon shoot
Beyond it and fall quivering on the field.
Dymer drew out his sword and raised the shield.

29

What now my friends? You get no more from me
Of Dymer. He goes from us. What he felt
Or saw from henceforth no man knows but he
Who has himself gone through the jungle belt
Of dying, into peace. That angel knelt
Far off and watched them close but could not see
Their battle. All was ended suddenly.

30

A leap—a cry—flurry of steel and claw,
Then silence. As before, the morning light
And the same brute crouched yonder; and he saw
Under its feet, broken and bent and white,
The ruined limbs of Dymer, killed outright
All in a moment, all his story done.
. . . But that same moment came the rising sun;

31

And thirty miles to westward, the grey cloud
Flushed into answering pink. Long shadows streamed
From every hill, and the low-hanging shroud
Of mist along the valleys broke and steamed
Gold-flecked to heaven. Far off the armour gleamed
Like glass upon the dead man's back. But now
The sentinel ran forward, hand to brow.

32

And staring. For between him and the sun
He saw that country clothed with dancing flowers
Where flower had never grown; and one by one
The splintered woods, as if from April showers,
Were softening into green. In the leafy towers
Rose the cool, sudden chattering on the tongues
Of happy birds with morning in their lungs.

33

The wave of flowers came breaking round his feet,
Crocus and bluebell, primrose, daffodil
Shivering with moisture: and the air grew sweet
Within his nostrils, changing heart and will,
Making him laugh. He looked, and Dymer still
Lay dead among the flowers and pinned beneath
The brute: but as he looked he held his breath;

34

For when he had gazed hard with steady eyes
Upon the brute, behold, no brute was there,
But someone towering large against the skies,
A wing'd and sworded shape, whose foam-like hair
Lay white about its shoulders, and the air
That came from it was burning hot. The whole
Pure body brimmed with life, as a full bowl.

35

And from the distant corner of day's birth
He heard clear trumpets blowing and bells ring,
A noise of great good coming into earth
And such a music as the dumb would sing
If Balder had led back the blameless spring
With victory, with the voice of charging spears,
And in white lands long-lost Saturnian years.

LAUNCELOT

LAUNCELOT

When the year dies in preparation for the birth
Of other seasons, not the same, on the same earth,
Then saving and calamity together make
The Advent gospel, telling how the heart will break
With dread, and stars, unleaving from the rivelled sky,
Scatter on the wind of man's Redemption drawing nigh,
Man's doom and his Redeeming and the wreck of man.
   Therefore it was in Advent that the Quest began;
In wail of wind the flower of the Britons all
Went out, and desolation was in Arthur's hall,   10
And stillness in the City of Legions. Then the Queen
Expected their returning when the woods were green;
But leaves grew large, and heaviness of August lay
Upon the woods. Then Guinever began to say,
'Autumn will bring them home again.' But autumn passed
With all its brown solemnities, and weathers fast
Came driving down the valley of the Usk with hail
At Advent, and the hearts of men began to fail,
And Lucan said, 'If summer brings the heathen men
From over-seas, or trouble of Picts beyond the wall,   20
Britain will break. The Sangrail has betrayed us all,
According to the prophecy Pelles the king
Once made, that at the moving of this holy thing
Our strength would fail.' But Arthur, who was daily less
Of speech, through all these winter days, gave answer,* 'Yes.
I know it, and I knew it when they rode away.'
   The year turned round and bettered, and the coloured May
Crept up the valley of the Usk, and softening green

* they say, this winter season, answered

[95]

Rounded the form of forests. But this year the Queen
Said nothing of the knight's return; and it became   30
A custom in that empty court never to name
The fear all felt, and not to listen any more
For rumours, nor to watch the roads, nor pace the shore;
Patience, most like conspiracy, had hushed them all,
Women, old men, and boys.
                                                     That year was heavy fall
Of snows. And when amid its silence Gawain, first
Defeat from the long Quest, came riding home, their thirst
For news he could not or he would not satisfy.
He was unlike the Gawain they had known, with eye   40
Unfrank, and voice ambiguous, and his answers short.
Gulfs of unknowing lay between him and the court,
Unbreakable misunderstandings. To the King,
He answered, No; he had not seen the holy thing.
And, No; he had heard no news of Launcelot and the rest,
But, for his own part, he was finished with the Quest
And now asked leave to journey North and see his own
Estates. And this was granted, and he went, alone,
Leaving a hollow-heartedness in every man
And, in the Queen, new fear. Then, with the spring, began   50
The home-coming of heroes from the Quest, by two's
And three's, unlike their expectations, without news,
A dim disquiet of defeated men, and all
Like Gawain, changed irrelevant in Arthur's hall,
Strange to their wives, unwelcome to the stripling boys.
Ladies of Britain mourned the losing of their joys:
'What have they eaten, or in what forgetful land
Were their adventures? Now they do not understand
Our speech. They talk to one another in a tongue
We do not know. Strange sorrows and new jests, among   60
Themselves, they have. The Sangrail has betrayed us all.'
So leaf by leaf the old fellowship of Arthur's hall
Felt Autumn's advent. New divisions came, and new
Allyings: till, of all the Table Round, those few
Alone who had not ridden on the dangerous Quest

Now bore the name of courteous and were loved the best
Mordred, or Kai, or Calburn, or Agravaine.
　　And the Queen understood it all. And the drab pain,
Now for two years familiar in her wearied side,
Stirred like a babe within her. Every nerve woke wide　　　　70
To torture, with low-moaning pity of self, with tears*
At dawn, with† midnight jealousies; and dancing fears
Touched with their stabs and quavers and low lingerings
Her soul, as a musician plays the trembling strings;
And loud winds from the cruel countries of despair
Came roaring through her, breaking down, and laying bare,
Till naked to the changing of the world she stood
At Advent. And no tidings now could do her good
Forever; the heart failing in her breast for fear
—Of Launcelot dead—of Launcelot daily drawing near　　　　80
And bringing her the sentence that she knew not of,
The doom, or the redeeming, or the change of love.
　　Yet, like a thief surprising her, the moment came
At last, of his returning. The tormented flame
Leaned from the candle guttering in the noisy gloom
Of wind and rain, where Guinever amid her room
Stood with scared eyes at midnight on the windy floor,
Thinking, forever thinking. From beyond her door
Came foot of sentry and change of countersign; and then
A murmur of their rough-mouthed talk between the men　　　　90
She heard, that in one moment like an arrow flew
Into the deepest crimson of her heart and slew
Hopes and half-doubts and self-deceits; and told the Queen
That Launcelot already had returned—had been
Three days now in the city and sent to her no word.
　　The rain was gone, the sky was pale, when next she stirred,
Having no memory of the passing of that night,
And in her cold, small fingers took her pen to write,
And wrote five words, and sent it by her aged nurse.

* *Lines 70-1 originally:*
　　Stirred like a babe within her *and woke; and* wide
　　　Prospects of woe and pits of deep dismay, with tears
　　　　　　† and

[97]

Then the cold hours began their march again, not worse,   100
Not better, never-ending. And that night he came,
Out of the doorway's curtained darkness to the flame
Of candlelight and firelight. And the curtains fell
Behind him, and they stood alone, with all to tell,
Not like that Launcelot tangled in the boughs of May
Long since, nor like the Guinever he kissed that day,
But he was pale, with pity in his face writ wide,
And she a haggard woman, holding to her side
A pale hand pressed, asking 'What is it?' Slowly then
He came to her and took her by the hand, as men   110
Take tenderly a daughter's or a mother's hand
To whom they bring bad news she will not understand.
So Launcelot led the Queen and made her sit: and all
This time he saw her shoulders move and her tears fall,
And he himself wept not, but sighed. Then, like a man
Who ponders, in the fire he gazed; and so began
Presently, looking always in the fire, the tale
Of his adventures seeking for the Holy Grail.

. . . How Launcelot and his shining horse had gone together
So far that at the last they came to springy weather;   120
The sharpened buds like lances were on every tree,
The little hills went past him like the waves of the sea,
The white, new castles, blazing on the distant fields
Were clearer than the painting upon new-made* shields.
Under high forests many days he rode, and all
The birds made shrill with marriage songs their shadowy hall
Far overhead. But afterwards the sun withdrew,
And into barren countries, having all gone through
The fair woods and the fortunate, he came at last.
He sees about him noble beeches overcast.   130
And aged oaks revealing to the rainless sky
Shagg'd nakedness of roots uptorn. He passes by
Forsaken wells and sees the buckets red with rust
Upon the chains. Dry watercourses filled with dust

* on new fashioned

[98]

He crosses over; and villages on every side
Ruined he sees, and jaws of houses gaping wide,
And abbeys showing ruinously the peeling gold
In roofless choirs and, underneath, the churchyard mould
Cracking and far subsiding into dusty caves
That let the pale light in upon* the ancient graves.   140
All day he journeys in a land of ruin and bones
And rags; and takes his rest at night among the stones
And broken things; till, after many leagues he found
A little stone-built hermitage in barren ground.
And at his door the hermit stands, so pined and thin
The bone-face is scarce hidden by the face of skin.
'Now fair, sweet friend,' says Launcelot, 'Tell me, I pray
How all this countryside has fallen into decay?'
The good man does not look on Launcelot at all,
But presently his loud, high voice comes like the call   150
Of a sad horn that blows to prayer in Pagan lands:
'This is the daughter of Babylon who gnaws her hands
For thirst and hunger. Nine broad realms in this distress
Are lying for the sake of one man's heedlessness
Who came to the King Fisherman, who saw the Spear
That burns with blood, who saw the Sangrail drawing near,
Yet would not ask for whom it served. Until there come
The Good Knight who will kneel and see, yet not be dumb,
But ask, the Wasted Country shall be still accursed
And the spell upon the Fisher King be unreversed,   160
Who now lies sick and languishing and near to death.'
So far the hermit's voice pealed on: and then his breath
Rattled within the dry pass of his throat: his head
Dropped sideways, and the slender trunk stands upright, dead,
And tall against the lintel of the narrow door.
And Launcelot alighted there, and in the floor
Of that low house scraped in the dust a shallow grave
And laid the good man in it, praying God to save
His soul; and for himself such grace as may prevail
To come to the King Fisherman and find the Grail.   170

* open

[99]

Then up he climbed and rode again, and from his breath
The dust was cleared, and from his mind the thought of death,
And in the country of ruin and rags he came so far
That over the grey moorland, like a shining star,
He sees a valley, emerald with grass, and gleam
Of water, under branches, from a winding stream,
A respite in the* wilderness, a pleasant place,
Struck with the sun. His charger sniffs and mends his pace,
And down† they go, by labyrinthine‡ paths, until
They reach the warm green country, sheltered by the hill.   180
Jargon of birds angelical warbles above,
And Launcelot throws his mail'd hood back, and liquid love
Wells in his heart. He looks all round the quartered sky
And wonders in what region Camelot may lie
Singing 'The breezes here have passed my lady's mouth
And stol'n a paradisal fragrance of the South.'
Singing 'All gentle hearts should worship her and sing
The praises of her pity and Fair-Welcoming.'
So carolling he trotted under lights and shadows
Of trembling woods, by waterfalls and sunny meadows,   190
And still he wandered, following where the water flows
To where, at the blue water's edge, a shrine arose
On marble pillars slender, with no wall between;
Through every arch the blueness of the sky was seen.
And underneath the fragile dome three narrow beds
Of lilies raised in windless air their silver heads.
Beside them sat a damosel, all clothed in bright,
Pale, airy clothes, and all her countenance filled with light,
And parted lips as though she had just ceased to sing.
Launcelot thinks he never has seen a fairer thing,   200
And checks his horse, saluting her. 'God send you bliss.
Beautiful one! I pray you tell, what place is this?'
The damsel said, 'The corseints in the praise of whom
This tomb is built are yet far distant from the tomb.
Here, when the Wasted Country is no longer dry,
The three best knights of Christendom shall come to lie.'

* Struck with the sun   † on   ‡ and down by winding

[100]

Launcelot remembers often to have heard them named
And guesses who is one of them: so half ashamed,
He asks her, with his eyes cast down, 'What knights are these?'
And waits; and then lifts up his eyes again, and sees   210
No lady there: an empty shrine, and on the grass
No print of foot, where in grey dew the blackbirds pass.
Then came on high a disembodied voice and gave
Solitude tongue. 'A grave for Bors,' it cried, 'A grave
For Percivale, a grave for Galahad: but not
For the Knight recreant of the Lake, for Launcelot!'
Then came clear laughter jingling in the air like bells
On horses' manes, thin merriment of that which dwells
In light and height, unaging and beyond the sense
Of guilt and grieving, merciless with innocence.   220
    And presently he catches up his horse's head
And rides again, still following where the water led.
The sun rose high: the shadow of the horse and man
Came from behind to underneath them and began
To lengthen out in front of them. The river flowed
Wider and always slower and the valley road
Was soft with mud, and winding, like a worm, between
Wide swamps and warm entanglement of puddles green;
And multitude of buzzing and of stinging flies
Came round his sweated forehead and his horse's eyes;   230
The black turf squeaked and trembled at the iron hoofs.
    Then Launcelot looks and sees a huddle of flat roofs
Upon a little island in the steaming land,
A low, red, Roman manor-house; and close at hand
A lady, riding softly on a mule, who came
Towards him, and saluted him, and told her name,
The Queen of Castle Mortal; but to Launcelot
Somewhat like Morgan the enchantress, and somewhat
Like Guinever, her countenance and talking seemed;
And golden, like a dragon's back, her clothing gleamed*   240
And courteously she prayed him, 'Since the night is near
Turn now and take your lodging in my manor here.'

                    * seemed

'Lady, may God repay you,' says the Knight, and so
Over the bridge, together, to the gate they go
And enter in. Young servitors enough he found
That kneeled before the lady, and came pressing round;
One took his helm, another took his spear, a third
Led off his horse; and chamberlains and grooms were stirred
To kindle fires and set him at the chimney side,
And clothe him in a long-sleeved mantle, soft and wide.   250
They go to dine. And presently her people all
Were gone away, he saw not where; and in the hall
He and the Lady sat alone. And it was night;
More than a hundred candles burned both still and bright.
His hostess makes great joy for him, and many a cup
Of strong wine, red as blood, she drinks; then rises up
And prays him bear her company and look on all
The marvels of her manor house. So out of hall,
Laughing, she leads him to the chapel-door: and when
That door was opened, fragrance such as dying men   260
Imagine in immortal countries, blown about
Heaven's meadows from the tree of life, came floating out.
No man was in the chapel, but he sees a light
There too of many hundred candles burning bright.
She led him in, and up into the choir, and there
He saw three coffins all of new cut stone, and fair
With flowers and knots, and full of spices to the brim
And from them came the odour that by now makes dim
His sense with deathly sweetness. But the heads of all
Those coffins passed beneath three arches in the wall.   270
On these he gazes; then on her. The sweet smell curls
About their brains. Her body is shaking like a girl's
Who loves too young; she has a wide and swimming eye;
She whispers him, 'The three best knights of earth shall lie
Here in my house'; and yet again, 'Lo, I have said,
The three best knights.' But Launcelot holds down his head,
And will not speak. 'What knights are these?' she said. And 'Nay.'
He answered, 'If you name them not, I dare not say.'
She laughed aloud—'A coffin for Sir Lamorake,

For Tristram; in the third lies Launcelot du Lake.'   280
He crossed himself and questioned her when these should die.
She answered, 'They shall all be living when they lie
Within these beds; and then—behold what will be done
To all, or even to two of them, or even to one,
Had I such grace.' She lifts her hand and turns a pin
Set on the wall. A bright steel blade drops down within
The arches, on the coffin-necks, so razor-keen
That scarce a movement of the spicey dust was seen
Where the edge sank. 'Ai! God forbid that you should be
The murderer of good knights,' said Launcelot. And she   290
Said, 'But for endless love of them I mean to make
Their sweetness mine beyond recovery and to take
That joy away from Morgan and from Guinever
And Nimue and Isoud and Elaine, and here
Keep those bright heads and comb their hair and make them lie
Between my breasts and worship them until I die.'

THE NAMELESS ISLE

In a spring season I sailed away
Early at evening of an April night.
Master mariner of the men was I,
Eighteen in all. And every day
We had weather at will. White-topped the seas
Rolled, and the rigging rang like music
While fast and fair the unfettered wind
Followed. Sometimes fine-sprinkling rain
Over our ship scudding sparkled for a moment
And was gone in a glance; then gleaming white   10
Of cloud-castles was unclosed, and the blue
Of bottomless heav'n, over the blowing waves
Blessed us returning. Half blind with her speed,
Foamy-throated, into the flash and salt
Of the seas rising our ship ran on
For ten days' time. Then came a turn of luck.
On the tenth evening too soon the light
Over working seas went beneath the sky line,
Darkness came dripping and the deafening storm
Upon wild waters, wet days and long,   20
Carried us, and caverned clouds immeasurable
Harried and hunted like a hare that ship
Too many days. Men were weary.
Then was a starless night when storm was worst,
The man of my mates whom most I loved
Cried 'Lost!' and then he leaped. Alive no more
Nor dead either the dear-loved face
Was seen. But soon, after his strange going,
Worse than the weathers, came the word shouted,
'Breakers ahead of us', and out of black darkness,   30
Hell-white, appeared horrid torment
Of water at the walls of a wild country.
The cliffs were high, cluttered with splinters

Of basalt at the base, bare-toothed. We found
Sea-room too small; we must split for sure,
And I heeded not the helm. Their hearts broke there,
The men I loved. Mad-faced they ran
All ways at once, till the waves swallowed
Many a smart seaman. Myself, I leaped
And wondered as I went what-like was death,   40
Before the cold clasped me. But there came a sea
Lifting from under me, so large a wave
That far above the foam of the first rock-shelves
It bore me, and far above the spray,
Upward, upward, into the air's region,
Beyond the cliffs into a yawning dark.
Other echoes, earthlier sounding,
In closer space, shut out the clamourous waves.
Then backward drawn with a babble of stones,
Softly sounding, in its spent fury,   50
A dull, dragging, withdrawing sigh,
That wave returned into the wastes, its home,
And would have sucked me back as I sank wearied,
But that there was grass growing where I gripped the land,
And roots all rough: so that I wrestled, clinging,
Against the water's tug. The wave left me,
And I grovelled on the ground, greatly wearied.

  How long I lay, lapped in my weariness,
Memory minds not. To me it seems
That for one full turn of the wheels above   60
I slept. Certainly when the sleep left me
There was calm and cool. No crashing of the sea,
But darkness all about. Dim-shadowed leaves
In mildest air moved above me,
And, over all, earth-scented smell
Sweetly stealing about the sea-worn man,
And faintly, as afar, fresh-water sounds,
Runnings and ripplings upon rocky stairs
Where moss grows most. Amidst it came,
Unearthly sweet, out of the air it seemed,   70

A voice singing to the vibrant string,
'Forget the grief upon the great water,
Card and compass and the cruel rain.
Leave that labour; lilies in the green wood
Toil not, toil not. Trouble were to weave them
Coats that come to them without care or toil.
Seek not the seas again; safer is the green wood,
Lilies that live there have labour not at all,
Spin not, spin not. Spent in vain the trouble were
Beauty to bring them that better comes by kind.'   80
　　Then I started up and stood, staring in the darkness,
After the closing strain. The clouds parted
Suddenly. The seemly, slow-gliding moon
Swam, as it were in shallows, of the silver cloud,
Out into the open, and with orb'd splendour
She gleamed upon the groves of a great forest.
There were trees taller than the topmost spire
Of some brave minster, a bishop's seat;
There very roots so vast that in
Their mossy caves a man could hide   90
Under their gnarl'd windings. And nearer hand
Ferns fathoms high. Flowers tall like trees,
Trees bright like flowers: trouble it is to me
To remember much of that mixed sweetness
The smell and the sight and the swaying plumes
Green and growing, all the gross riches,
Waste fecundity of a wanton earth,*
—Gentle is the genius of that juicy wood,—
Insatiable the soil. There stood, breast high,
In flowery foam, under the flame of moon,   100
One not far off, nobly fashioned.
Her beauty burned in my blood, that, as a fool,
Falling before her at her feet I prayed,
Dreaming of druery, and with many a dear craving
Wooed the woman under the wild forest.
She laughed when I told my love-business,

* sail

[109]

Witch-hearted queen. 'A worthy thing,
Traveller, truly, my troth to plight
With the sea villain that smells of tar
Horny-handed, and hairy-cheeked.'   110
Then I rose wrathfully; would have ravished the witch
In her empty isle, under that orb'd splendour.
    But she laughed louder, and a little way
She went back, beckoning with brows and eyes.
Like to* lilies, when she loosed her robe
Under broad† moonshine, her breasts appeared,
No maiden's breasts, but with milk swelling,
Like Rhea unrobed, rich in offspring.
Her sign was not sent to the sea-wanderer:
Others answered. From the arch'd forest   120
Beasts came baying: the bearded ape,
The lion, the lamb, the long-sided,
Padding panther, and the purring cat,
The snake sliding, and the stepping horse,
Busy beaver, and the bear jog-trot,
The scurrying **rat,** and the squirrel leaping
On the branch above. Those beasts came all.
She grudged no grace to those grim ones. I
Saw how she suckled at her sweet fountains
The tribes that go dumb. Teeth she feared not,   130
Her nipple was not denied to the nosing worm.
I thought also that out of the thick foliage
I saw the branches bend towards her breast, thirsting,
Creepers climbing and the cups of flowers
Upward opening—all things that lived,
As for sap, sucking at her sweet fountains.
And as the wood milked her, witch-hearted queen,
I saw that she smiled, softly murmuring
As if she hushed a child. How long it was
These marvels stood, memory holds not,   140
—All was gone in a glance. Under the green forest
We two were alone, as from trance wakened.

She was far fairer than at the first seeing.
Then she struck the string and sang clearly
Another lay. Earth stood silent.
'You are too young in years. My yesterdays,
Left behind me, are a longer tale
Than your histories hold. Far hence she lies
Who would learn gladlier of your love-business.
Woven in wizardry, wearily she lingers,   150
Stiller and stiller, with the stone in her heart,
Crying; so cruelly creeps the bitter change on her,
—Happy the head is that shall harbour in that breast—
My dear daughter, that dieth away,
In the enchanter's chain. Who chooses best
Will adventure his life and advance far on
Into the cruel country. If he comes again
Bringing that beautiful one, out of bonds redeemed,
He shall win for reward a winsome love.'
'This quarrel and quest, Queen,' I answered,   160
'I will undertake though I earn my death
At the wizard's wiles. But of the way thither,
The councils, and the kind, of the crafty man,
Tell me truly.' When she turned her face
Her teeth glittered. She tossed her head,
Nostrils widened, as a noble dame
In scorn, scoffing, at a shameful thing*—
'Eastward in the island the old one stands
Working wonders in the woful shade
Of a grim garden that is growing there   170
Newly planted. That was the navel once
Of a sweet country, stol'n now from me,
Where he would be called a king. But he is cold at heart
And he has wrought ruin in those rich pleasances,
He has felled forests, put to flight my beasts,
Chaining with enchantment many a changeful stream,
Putting into prison all that his power reaches;
Life is loathsome to† that lord; and joy,

* scandal. Then;   † For life is loathed by

[111]

Abomination; and the bed of love
Eggs him with envy—outcast himself,   180
An old, ugly, ice-hearted wraith.
If I saw shaking the skin upon his throat,
Or the rheum dropping from his red eyelids,
Or his tongue mumbling in the toothless gums,
By loathing I should lose my life. Strong thief!
Once amid these waters, well was my country,
Living lonely in my land, a queen.
Truly, I cannot tell of a time before
I was ruling this realm. I am its right lady.
Ages after, that other came   190
Out of the ocean in an hour of storm,
Humble and homeless. At my hearth, kneeling,
Sweetly he besought me to save his life,
And grant him ground where he might grow his bread.
All that he asked for, ill-starred I gave,
Pleased with pity, that I have paid dearly,
And easily won. But for each acre
That my bounty gave to the beggar, soon
He stole a second, till as a strong tyrant
He holds in his hand one half the land.   200
My flute he has stolen. Flowers loved it well
And rose upright at the ripple of the note
Sound-drenched, as if they drank,* after drought, sweet rain.
Grass was the greener for it, as at grey evening
After the sun's setting of a summer day,
When dusk comes near, and the drooping, crushed
Stalks stand once more in the still twilight.
That reed of delight he ravished away,
Stole it stealthily. In a strange prison
It lies unloved; and of my life one half   210
With the flute followed, and I am faded now,
Mute the music. But a mightier woe
Followed the first one; with his fine weavings,
Cobwebby, clinging, and his cruel, thin

* drinking

[112]

Enchanter's chains, he has charmed away
My only child out of my own country,
Into the grim garden, and will give her to drink
Heart-changing draughts.* He that tastes of them
Shall stand, a stone, till the stars crumble.
Of that drug drink not, lest, in his danger caught,   220
Moveless as marble thou remain. But take
This sword, seaman, and strike off his head.
Hasten, if haply, ere his hard threatenings
Or his lies' labyrinth, lapped about her,
Have driven her to drink that draught, in time,
You may redeem my dear.'
                                    Dawn was round me,
Cool and coloured, and there came a breeze
Brushing the grasses. Birds were chattering.
There was I only in the empty wood,   230
The woman away. One time I thought
It was a dream's burden; but, amid the dews sprinkled
At my feet, flashing, that fallow sword
Lay to my liking. Lingeringly I weighed it,
Bright and balanced. That was the best weapon
That ever I owned. I ate in that place
My full upon the fruits the forest bore.
Then, among still shadows, slow-paced I went
Always eastward into the arch'd forest.
It was at the fifth furlong, forth I issued   240
From the dreaming wood into a down country.
All the island opened like a picture
Before my feet. Far-off the hills,
Long and limber, as it were lean greyhounds,
With level chines, lay beneath the sunrise.
Chalk made them pale. Never a church nor a rick
Nor smoke, nor the smell of a small homestead,
Rose upon the ridges. The rolling land
Climbed to the eastward—there was the clearest sky—
Heaving ever hillward, until high moorland   250

* brews

[113]

Shut off my seeing. The sorcerer's home,
My goal, was there as I guessed. Thither
I held my way and my heart lightened.
   Over hedge, over ditch, over high, over low,
By waters and woods I went and ran,
And swung the sword as I swung my legs.
Laughing loudly, alone I walked,
Till many a mile was marched away.
   Half-way in heav'n to his highest throne
The gold sun glittering had gained above,   260
When I looked and lo!, in the long grasses
By a brook's margin a bright thing lay,
Reflecting the flame of floating sun,
Drawing my glances. As in danger, aside
I swerved in my step: a serpent I thought
Basking its belly in the bright morning
Lay there below me. But when I looked again,
Lo it never moved. Nearer gazing,
I found it was a flute, fashioned delicately,
Purely golden. When I picked it up   270
I could make with my mouth no music at all
And with my five fingers, failing always
Whatever tune I tried, testing that instrument.
Almost, in anger—for it irked me so—
I had flung the flute among the flowers and grass,
Let it lie there by the lapping stream.
Presently I put it in the pouch I bear
Set on my shoulder. It was my second thoughts.
   Over hedge, over ditch, over high, over low,
By waters and woods I went and ran,   280
And swung the sword as I swung my legs.
Laughing loudly alone I walked,
Till many a mile was marched away.
   Bright above me on the bridge of noon
Sun was standing, shadows dwindled,
Heat was hovering in a haze that danced
Upon rocks about my road. I raised my eyes.

[114]

On the green bosom of a* grassy hill,
White, like wethers, in a wide circle,
Stones were standing; as on Salisbury Plain   290
Where wild men made for the worshipt sun
That old altar. On thither I went
Marching right among them. Man-shaped they were,
Now that I was nearer and could know their kind,
—Awful images, as it were an earlier race,
Nearer neighbours of the noble gods,
They were so quiet and cold. Kingly faces
There hushed my heart from its hard knockings.

    As I walked, wondering, in their wide consistory,
Through and through them, for the throng was great,   300
Fear stopped my breath. I found sitting
Lonely among the lifeless, but alive, a man,
His head hanging, and his hands were clasped,
His arms knotted, and from his eyes there came,
Sadly, without ceasing, slow tears and large.
Hunched and hairy was his whole body,
Durned and dwindled. Dwarflike he seemed,
But his ears bigger than any other man's.
He was grubby as if he had grown from the ground, plantlike,
Big of belly, and with bandy legs.   310
Shrublike his shape, shocked-headed too,
As if a great gooseberry could go upon legs,
Or a mangel be a man. Amazed, I spoke.
'What little wight then, weeping among the stonemen,
Lives alone here? What is the load of care
That has dwelled in you, dwarf, and dwined you thus?'
Then the little man lifted up his eyebrows
And he spoke sadly. 'Sorrow it is to me
To remember my mates. Men they were born
Who are now stone-silenced in this circle here,   320
By wizard's wand. Once they beat me,
Captain kicked me, and cook also,
Bosun boxed me on both my ears,

                    * the

                    [115]

Cabin-boy, carpenter—all the crew of the *Well Away*—
Before they fell—she foundered here—
Into the wizard's hand. He worked them into stone,
That they move no more, on the main or on the shore.
Able seaman of old were they all,
Ranting and roaring when the rum was in
Like true British sailors. Trouble it is to me   330
To remember my mates—the men that they were!
I shall not meet their match. When the mate was drunk
It took all ten of their toughest men
In a strange seaport to shut him up.
Now they are stones, standing. He stopped their life,
Made them into marble, and of more beauty,
Fairer faces, and their form nobler,
Proud and princely. But the price was death.
They have bought beauty. That broke my heart.'
'I am an enemy to that old sorcerer,   340
Dwarf,' I answered. 'Dwelling in the greenwood
Where the waves westward wash the sea-cliff,
I found, fairest of all flesh, the Queen
Who should rule this realm, for she is its right lady.
I am sent on her side. I shall save the land
From the enchanter's chain; so my charge bids me.
Lead me loyally where that lord dwelleth
In his ill garden, ice-hearted man.'
      The dwarf answered 'She who dwells in the wood
Is the second fear in this strange country.   350
She has a wand also, that woman there;
Whom she chooses to change, she'll choke the voice
In his throat. Thickly, like a thing without sense,
Growling and grunting, grovelling four-foot,
He will pad upon paws. Pelt coats him round,
He is a brute beast then, once her bonds catch him.
The other half of my old shipmates
She bewitched in her wood. It is the way she deals.
Therefore I lurk alone in the land between
Twixt the devil and the deep. I am in dread of both,   360

Either the stone or the sty. But here I stay, hoping
Always, if ever such an hour should come.
To drink before I die out of the deep tankard,
And to eat ham and eggs in my home country
That is the weald of Kent. And I wish that I was there.'
   Doubts came darkening and all grew dull within,
Cold and clouded with clinging dread,
At this new story. Noon was burning
Bright about us. I bade the dwarf
To lead me, though he was loth, to the lair of the mage.   370
Willingly he would not. But with word of threat,
With coaxing and with kicks, he must come at the last,
Following me; a faltering, faint-hearted guide.
   Over hedge, over ditch, over high, over low,
By waters and wood I went and ran
Till many a mile was marched away.
I swung no more my sword as I walked;
Little stomach to laugh had I,
And shuffling, and shaking on his shoulders his shaggy head came the
    dwarf,
Cunningly catching all occasions to creep aside out of the way.   380
Every mile, he would be asking for another rest. If I had let him,
The task would have been interminable, the tale wanted an ending.
Day was dropping to the dazzling plain
Of the waves westward. Winging homeward
Came the flying flocks; flowers were closing,
Level light over the land was poured.
I looked to my left in a low valley
Among quiet flowers. Queen-like there stood
A marble maid, mild of countenance,
Her lips open, her limbs so lithe   390
Made for moving, that the marble death
Seemed but that moment to have swathed her round.
Her beauty made me bow as a brute to the earth.
To have won a word of her winsome mouth,
Scorn or sweetness, salutation,
Bidding or blessing, I would have borne great pain.

Longing bade me to lay my cheek
On the cool, carven countenance, and worshipping
To kiss the maid, if so she might come awake.
Awe forbade me, and her anger feared.   400
Then I was ware in a while of one behind;
There stood in stole that stately fell
And swept, beneath, the sward, a man.
The beard upon his bos'm, burnt-gold in hue
Grew to his girdle. That was the gravest man,
Of amplest brow, and his eye steadiest,
And his mien mightiest, that I have have met in earth.
Then I gathered more sure my grip upon the sword,
And for clear arm-play I cast aside
From shoulder my sack. The silly dwarf   410
Caught and kept it. He was cold at heart
Whimpering and woebegone. The wizard spoke:
    'Second counsels, my son, are best.
If my art aid not, in empty land,
Lonely and longing for a lifeless stone,
Here you may harbour. What help is that?
Marble minds not a man's desire,
Cold lips comfort him neither with kiss nor speech,
Nor will her arms open. Eager lover,
Not even the art of this old master   420
Can wake, as you want, this woman here.
Chaste, enchanted, till the change of the world,
In beauty she abides. Nor breath, nor death,
Touches nor troubles her. You can be turned and made
Nearer to her nature; not she to yours
Ever. Only your own changing,
Boy, can bring you, where your bride waits you,
If you are love-learned to so large a deed.
You think, being a thrall, that it is thorough death
To be made marble and to move no limb.   430
Wise men are wary. Once only fools
Look before leaping. Lies were told you.

Fear was informer;* else you had freely craved,
If your master had been love, to be made even now
Like to the Lady. It was your loins told you,
And your belly, and your blood, and your blind servants
Five, who are unfaithful. Fear had moved them.
Death they were in dread of. Death let them have;
For their fading and their fall is the first waking,
And their night the noon, of a new master,   440
Peace after pleasure. Passionless for the stonemen†
Life stands limpid. Left far behind
Is that race rushing over its roar'd cataracts,
The murmuring, mixed, much thwarted stream
Of the flesh, flowing with confused noise,
Perishing perpetually. Had you proved one hour
Their blessed life whose blood is stilled,
—How they hearken to the heavens raining
Starry influence in the still of night,
Feel the fingers, far below them   450
Of the earth's archon in an ancient place
Moulding metals: how among them steals,
As the moon moves them when the month flows full,
Love and longing, that is unlike mortals'
Dreams of druery, drawn from further,
Nobler in nature—you would know 'tis small
Wonder if they will not to wander any more.
Life has left them, whoso looks without;
All things are other on their inner side.
This child that I have changed with the chalice of peace,   460
Was my own daughter. I, pondering much,
Gave her the greatest of gifts I knew.
Long she was in labour in a land of dread,
Tangled in torments. The toils had her,
And her wild mother, witch-hearted queen,
Delayed her in that lair. Long since it was
When the woman was my wife. Worse befell her
After, when she was evil. By arts she stole

* You belly [*illegible*]   † among them

[119]

The golden flute, that was a gift fashioned
For my dear daughter, and a daemon's work,   470
The earth's archon of old made it.
She took the toy. To touch the stops
Or to make with her mouth the music it held,
Art she had not. Envy moved her.
She was changed at heart. My child she stole,
Fled to the forests: found there comrades,
Beasts and brambles and brown shadows,
With whom she holds. Half this island
Wrongly she has ravished. I am its rightful lord.
Where she flung the flute as she fled thither,   480
No man knoweth. None the richer
Was the thief of her theft: but that she thinks it wealth
If another ail. She aches at heart.
Second counsels, oh son, are best.
All things are other on their inner side.'
    He spoke those words. They sped so well,
What for the maiden's love and the man's wisdom,
Awed and eager, I asked him soon
For a draught of that drink. Drought parched my throat.
Cold and crystal in the cup it glanced,   490
White like water. In the west, scarlet,
Day was dying. Dark night apace
Over* earth's eastern edge towards us
Came striding up. Stars, one or two,
Had lit their lamps. My lip was set
To the cold border of the cup. The dwarf
Cried out and crossed himself: 'This is a crazy thing!
Dilly, dilly, as the duckwife said,
Come and let me kill you. Catch younger trouts, Sir,
Tickling, tickling, with no trouble at all.'   500
    'What meddling mite,' said the man of spells,
'Creeps in my country? Clod! Earth thou art,
Unworthy to be worked to a white glory
Of stable stone. But stay not long,

* Of

[120]

Base, mid thy betters! Or into boggy peats,
Slave, I'll sing thee.' But he skipped away
Light and limber, though his limbs were crook'd.
Out of the bag that he bore on his brown shoulder
—He had caught it and kept when I cast it away—
The dwarf deftly* drew the flute out,   510
Gold and glittering. Grinned while he spoke,
'All things, ogre, have another side.
I trust even now, by a trick I have learnt,
That I shall drink before I die out of a deep tankard
In the weald of Kent, will you, nill you!'
He laid his lip to the little flute.
Long and liquid,—light was waning—
The first note flowed. Then faster came,
Reedily, ripple-like, running as a watercourse,
Meddling of melodies, moulded in air,   520
Pure and proportional. Pattering as the rain-drops
Showers of it, scattering silverly, poured on us,
Charmed the enchanter that he was changed and wept,
At the pure, plashing, piping of the melody,
Coolly calling, clearer than a nightingale,
Defter and more delicate. Dainty the division of it,
True the trilling and the turns upon itself,
Sweet the descending. For it sang so well,
First he fluted off his flesh away
The shaggy hair; and from his shoulders next   530
Heaved by harmonies the hump away;
Then he unbandied, with a burst of beauty, his legs,
Standing straighter as the strain loudened.
I saw that the skin was smoother on his face
Than a five-year boy's. He was the fairest thing
That ever was on earth. Either shoulder
Was swept with wings; swan's down they were,
Elf-bright his eyes. Evening darkened,
The sun had set. Over the sward he danced,
With arms open, as an eager boy   540

* Deftly the dwarf

[121]

Leaps towards his lover. I looked whither.
Noble creatures were coming near, and more
Stirring, as I saw them, out of stone bondage,
Stirring, and descending from their still places,
And every image shook, as an egg trembles
Over the breaking beak. Through the broad garden
—The dew drenched it—drawn, ev'n as moths,
To that elf's glimmering, his old shipmates
Moved to meet him. There, among, was tears,
Clipping and kissing. King they hailed him,   550
Men, once marble, that were his mates of old,
Fair in feature and of form godlike,
For the stamp of the stone was still on them
Carved by the wizard. They kept, and lived,
The marble mien. They were men weeping,
Round the dwarf dancing to his deft fingers.
Then was the grey garden as if the gods of heaven
On the carol dancing had come and chos'n
The flowers folded, for their floor to dance.
Close beside me, as when a cloud brightens   560
When, mid thin vapours, through comes the sun,
The marble maid, under mask of stone,
Shook and shuddered. As a shadow streams
Over the wheat waving, over the woman's face
Life came lingering. Nor was it long after
Down its blue pathways, blood returning
Moved, and mounted to her maiden cheek.
Breathing broadened her breast. Then light
From her eyes' opening all that beauty
Worked into woman. So the wonder was complete,   570
Set, precipitate, and the seal taken,
Clear and crystal the alchemic change,
Bright and breathing. In my breast faltering
My spirit was spent. Speech none I found,
Standing by* the stranger who was stone before.
But the wing'd wonder—wide rings they danced

* before

[122]

Over the flowers folded to his fluting sweet—
Danced to my dear one. Druery he taught her,
Bent her, bowed her, bent never before,
Brought her, blushing as it were a bride mortal, 580
To hold to her heart my head as I kneeled,
Faint in that ferly: frail, mortal man,
Till I was love-learnëd both to learn and teach
Love with that lady. Nor was it long after
That the man of spells moved and started
As one that wakes. 'Weary it is to me
To remember much. Miseries innumerable
Have ruled in this realm. I will run quickly
West to the woodland, to the wild city,
Haply my love lives yet. Long time I've borne 590
Hate and hungering. Now is harvest come,
Now is the hour striking, the ice melting,
The bond broken, and the bride waiting.'
    All in order—the old one led—
On flowers folded, to flute music,
Forth we followed. No fays lightlier
Dance and double in their dew'd ringlet
On All Saints Eve. Earth-breathing scents
On mildest breeze moved towards us.
Cobwebs caught us. Clear-voiced, an owl 600
To his kind calling clove the darkness,*
The fox, further, was faint barking.
We came quickly to the country of downs
That lies so long between the land of dread
And the grim garden. Glory breaking
Unclosed the clouds. Clear and golden
Out into the open swam the orb'd splendour
Of a moon, marvellous. Magic called her.
Pale as paper, where she poured her ray
The downs lay drenched. Dark before us, 610
Stilly standing, was the stern frontier
Of the aisled forest. Out thence there came

* night sky

[123]

Thunder, I thought it. Thick copses broke.
From dread darkness, with drumming hoofs,
Swept the centaurs, swift in onset,
Abreast, embattled, as a broad army,
To that elf's glimmering. They were his old shipmates,
Unenchanted, as those others were,
Bettered after beasthood. They had the brows of men,
Tongues to talk with, and, to touch the string,   620
Hands for harping. But the horse lingered,
And the mark of their might, as magic had wrought,
The stamp of that strength was still on them.
Hands for harping, hoofs for running,
Mighty stallions, that were men weeping
Round the dwarf dancing to his deft music.
First before them ran the fairest one,
Comeliest of the coursers; king-like his eye,
Proud his pawing and his pomp of speed,
Big and bearded. On his back riding—   630
Such courtesy he could—there came, so fair,
The lady of the land, lily-breasted,
Gentle and rejoicing. The magician's love
Made her beauty burn as a bright ruby
Or as a coal on fire, under cool moonlight,
And swam in her eyes till she swooned almost
Bending her body to his back on whom she rode.
And now full near those nations stood,
That king's courtiers whom he had carved in stone,
And the wide flung wings of the woman's horse,   640
Both as for battle; all the beauty of his,
The strength of hers. Straightway they fell
To talk, those two. Their tale was sweet
In all our ears. Earth stood silent.
Either answered other softly.
HIC: 'My love's laughter is light falling
Through broad branches in brown woodland,
On a cold fountain, in a cave darkling,
A mild sparkling in mossy gloom.'

ILLA: 'But my lord's wisdom is light breaking,   650
And sound shaking, a sundered tomb.'
HIC: 'My love's looking is long dimness
And stars' influence. In strange darkness
Her eyes open their orb'd dreaming
As a huge, gleaming* mid-harvest moon.'
ILLA: 'But my lord's looking is the lance darted
Through mists parted when morn comes soon.'
HIC: 'Thy dear bosom is a deep garden
Between high hedges where heat burns not,
Where no rains ruin and no rimes harden,   660
A closed garden, where climbs no snake.'
ILLA: 'But thy dear valour is a deep, rolling,
And a tower tolling strong towns awake.'
HIC: 'My friend's beauty is the free springing
Of the world's welfare from the womb'd ploughland,
The green growing, the great mothering,
Her breast smothering with her brood unfurled.'
ILLA: 'But my friend's beauty is the form minted
Above heav'n, printed on the holy world.'
   So they were singing. The song was done.   670
When either in arms other folded
Fondly and fairly, fire-red was she,
Fire-white the sage. The fields of air
Beamed more brightly. About the moon
More than a myriad mazy weavings
Of fire flickered. Far off there rolled
Summer thunder. The sage all mild
For the maid and for me his mouth opened,
   'The air of earth this other two
Must breathe in breast. Now broad ocean   680
Smiles in sleeping and smoother winds
Favour, let us find them a ferry hence.
This elf also, even as he wished for,
Hoping, while he was helpless, for his home country,
Earth of England, unenchanted,

                    * huge-seeming

                       [125]

Let us send on the sea. He served us well,
MULTUM AMAVIT, which is of most virtue,
In heav'n and here and in hell under us.'
    Centaurs swiftly, when he said, were gone,
Glorying in gallop to the great forest.   690
Heaving hardily, whole trees they tore
From earth upward. Echoing ruin
Dinned in darkness. Down thence they hauled
Many an ancient oak. The orb'd splendour
Shone on their shoulders as they sweat naked
Under moon's mildness. Magic helped them,
The boat was built in the blink of an eye,
Long and limber, of line stately,
Fair in fashion. Out of the forest came
Spiders for spinning, speedily they footed,   700
Shooting like shuttles on the shadowy grass,
Backward and forward, brisk upon their spindle shanks,
And made for the mast a marvellous sail
Of shimmering wèb. That ship full soon
Over grass gliding, glorious stallions
With Heave! and Ho! hauled to the sea's rim,
A throng, dancing. They thrust her out
Into deep water. There was din of hoofs
In salt shallows and the spray cast up
Under moon, glancing. The maiden soon,   710
The elf also, I then, the third,
Were on board in the boat. Breathing mildly
Off the island,—it arched our sail—
The breeze blew then, blest the fragrance*
Of flower and fruit, floating seaward,
Land-laden air. I long even now
To remember more of that mixed sweetness.
But fast and fair into the foamless bay
Onward and outward, under the orb'd splendour,
Our boat was borne. Back oft I gazed†   720

      * stealing
     † Backward gazing

As the land lessened, lo!, all that folk
Burned on the beaches as they were bright angels,
Light and lovely, and the long ridges
With their folds fleecy under the flame of moon
Swam in silver of swathing mist,
Elf-fair that isle. But on apace
We went on the wave. That winged boy
Held firm the helm. Ahead, far on,
Like floor unflawed, the flood, moon-bright,
Stretched forth the twinkling streets of ocean   730
To the rim of the world. No ripple at all
Nor foam was found, save the furrow we made,
The stir at our stern, and the strong cleaving
Of the throbbing prow. We thrust so swift,
Moved with magic, that a mighty curve
Upward arching from either bow
Rose, all rainbowed; as a rampart stood
Bright about us. As the book tells us,
Walls of water, and a way between,
Were reared and rose at the Red Sea ford,   740
On either hand, when Israel came
Out of Egypt to their own country.

THE QUEEN OF DRUM

A Story in Five Cantos

CANTO I

I

(Quick! The last chance! The dawn will find us.
Look back! How luminous that place
—We have come from there. The doors behind us
Swing close and closer, the last trace
Vanishes. Quick! Let no awaking
Wash out this memory. Mark my face,
Know me again—join hands—it's breaking—
Remember—wait!—know me . . .)

                          Remember whom?
Who is there? Who answered? Empty, the cold gloom   10
Before the daybreak, when the moon has set.
It's over. It was a dream. They will forget.

II

To the King of Drum,* at last, beyond pretence
Of sleep, the day returned, the inevitable sense
Of well-known things around him: on the ceiling
The plaster-gilt rosettes crumbling, the lilies peeling.
Gentlemen, pages, lords, and flunkey things
In lace who act the nurse to lonely kings,
Tumbled his poor old bones somehow from bed.
Swallowing their yawns, whispering with louted head,   20
Passed him from hand to hand, tousled and grey
And blinking like an owl surprised by day,
Rubbing his bleary eyes, muttering between dry gums
                    * To the guarded king

'Gi' me my teeth . . . dead tired . . . my lords—''t all comes
From living in the valley. Too much wood.
Sleep the clock round in Drum and get no good.'

III

Now half they had dressed the King, half made him dress.
And day's long steeplechase one jump the less
Unrolled ahead (night's pillows and the star
Of night no more immeasurably far).   30
   Now the long passage* where the walls are thick
As in the Egyptian tombs, echoes his stick
Tapping the cold, grey floor. There, at his side,
With sharp, unlooked for sound, a door flung wide
As from impatient hands, and tall, between
The swing of the flung curtains, stepped the Queen.
—'So fast, Madam? Young limbs are supple, eh?
And easily get their rest. I'll dare to say
You have been abroad by night—not known your bed
More than an hour. Is it true?'   40
                And when she said
Nothing at all, he tapped the ground, and nearing,
Knowingly, his big grey face to hers, and peering,
Screwed home the question, snarling. And she stood
And never spoke. She too was tired, the blood
Drained from her quiet cheek. Wind-broken skies
Had havocked in her hair, and in her eyes
Printed their reckless image. Coldest grey
Those eyes, and sharp† of sight from far away:
More bright a little, something steadier than   50
Man cares to meet with in the face of man
Or woman; alien eyes. For one unbroken
Big moment's silence, swift as rain, unspoken
Questions went to and fro, and edged replies
Flitting like motes from their embattled eyes

* The unending
† clear

—(Out of the neighbouring past, an unlaid fear
Signals its fellows, calls 'I am here. I am here.'
Whispers the King, 'Touch not, lest it should wake
The enormous tooth that once has ceased to ache.')
Till with a shrug, turning, he first withdrew   60
His gaze, yet softly breathed, 'You . . . Maenad, you!'

IV

That heavy day the servants had been late
Setting to rights the carven room of state
Where council met. Bucket and mop were there
Still, and the smell of soot was in the air,
And half-awakened, chilly footmen cursed
And justled yet, as, one by one, the first
And youngest of the Notables of Drum
Came straggling in;* spiritless all, all dumb,
As men who with their first awakening yawn   70
Had sipped an added loathing for the dawn,
Thinking 'The Council sits to-day.'
                                        And then,
—Long intervals between—the older men,
With more important frowns that seemed to claim
Business of state for pretext, drifting came
Down the long floor like arctic bergs afloat,
With rustling gowns, with clearing of the throat,
Bark of defiant cough, official sound
Of papers spread, and testy glance around.   80

V

Now at the long green board they are seated all
In the very old carved room, so thick of wall,
So narrow-windowed, here, an hour from noon,
Men work by lamplight in the month of June.

* there

[133]

The oldest of them all play noughts and crosses,
A gambler reckons up his evening losses.
One trims his nails, one spreads his hands and lays
A bright, bald head between them on the baize.
The General, his big lips distanced wide,
Fumbles with half a hand concealed inside,   90
Picking a tooth. The Chancellor, with head
Close to the paper and quick-moving lead,
Sketches and strokes all out and draws again
Angular pigs, straight trees, and armless men.
More peaceful far beside him in his place
The Lord Archbishop nods: a rosy face
Cherubically dimpled, settling down
Each moment further into beard and gown
—Into foamed, silvery beard and snowy bands;
Folded, on quiet breast, his baby hands   100
—Smooth, never-laboured hands, calm, happy heart,
Like sculptures monumentally at rest
On some cathedral tomb.
    Then suddenly a* stir runs down the room,
—The crumbling of scrawled paper, and the shake
Hurriedly given to jog a friend awake,
Scraping of chairs, quick gabbled finishing
Of whispered tales. Men rise to meet the King.

                            VI

Heavily the hours, like laden barges passed
—Motion, amendment, order, motion. Now at last   110
The trickling current of the slow debate
Sets towards that ocean sea, where soon or late
Time out of mind their consultations come,
—The everlasting theme 'What's wrong with Drum?'
When, marvellous to dull'd ears, elf-bright between
Two droning wastes of talk, one name—'The Queen'
Broke startling. And the scribbler dropped the pen
And sleepers rubbed their eyes and whispering men
                        * the

[134]

Drew heads apart watching.
                           Yes. Sure enough.   120
The Chancellor's on his feet and taking snuff
And writhing and grimacing with a bow
In the article of deprecation . . . . Now,
Listen!
          . . . 'and also seen by vulgar eyes
In her most virtuous, yet, perhaps, unwise
Occasions' . . . 'a King's house contains the weal
Of all. He is the axle of the wheel,
The root of the politic tree, the fountain's spring.' . . .
'Nothing is wholly private in a King.   130
For what more private to each man alone
Than health, my lords? Yet, if the monarch groan,
The duteous subject.' . . . *
                           . . . 'dutifully rude,
Without offence, offending, must intrude'
And 'Kings to their own majesty resign
The privacy, my lords, that yours and mine' . . .
(Hist! Now it's coming)
                           . . . 'in a private woman
'Twere not convenient: for a queen, inhuman.   140
Thus to expose a teeming nation's care
And princes yet unborn, to the damp air
Of middle night, and fogs—the common curse
Of our low land—besides, my lords, what worse
May haunt such place and time. As well, you have heard,
All of you, how injuriously the word
Of these things runs abroad. The people know!
Always some chattering dame has seen her go
Past midnight, and on foot, beyond the gates
Out hill-wards, when the frost upon the slates   150
Winked to the moon . . . then, the same week, another

* subject'. . . .
          Lost, once more, the thread . . .
     Something like 'fans the brow' and 'fevered head',
     Then 'rough affection' . . . 'dutifully . . .

Has gossipped with a country girl, whose brother,
—Some forester—by night, in wind and rain,
Past three o'clock of the morn, time and again,
Plodding his homeward journey in the jaws
Of darkness, where the gust in dripping shaws
Blows out his lantern, swears he has often seen
Straight in his path, and like a ghost, the Queen,
—Scaring him: as he kneeled to kiss her hand
Brushing him by, so soft.   160
                          Cloud in the land
Nature has given enough: but this is cloud
Deeper than darkness, cold as death's own shroud,
Poisoning the people's thought. You must command
Where counsel fails. You, Sire, with sceptred hand,
With royal brow—stamp out the infected thing
. . . And merge, at least, the husband in the King.'
    But as he ended, from the lowest place
At the board's end, a screeching raw-boned boy
Jumps up, with hair like flax, and freckled face,   170
And knuckley fingers working with the joy
Of having found his tongue—'My lords, they say
Far more than this . . . and worse . . . they say . . . the sounds
And lights along the mountains far away
At night . . . and then she's on her hunting grounds
With all of those . . . they . . . you—you have fobbed them off
And lied to them . . .'
                          —but babble and loud cough,
Laughter and plucking hands and stare and frown
Had covered the boy's speech and pulled him down,   180
While lowly boomed the General, 'Odds my life.
Damn nonsense. Have a wife and rule a wife.
Woman—they say—and dog—and walnut tree—
More you beat'm—better they be—'
When, gradually, a stir about the door,
A sense of things amiss, then more and more
A patch of silence, dimly felt,* that spread
                    * felt not heard

[136]

In widening circles from the table's head,
Turned thither all their eyes, all ears to wait
The word of the King: who from his chair of state   190
Half rising (in his hand a paper shook)
Laboured, faltering, to speech, with shifty look
Settling towards blank dismay. 'My lords—she's here—
My lords, the Queen—has something for your ear—
Craves entry.'
            And across those champions all
Change passed, as when the sunlight leaves the wall.

VII

And all at once the Queen was there,
A flash of eyes, a flash of hair,
Nostril widened, teeth laid bare,   200
Omens of her breathing, and
Robe caught breastward in one hand,
Tall mid their seated shapes: a hush
Of moments:* then the torrent rush
Of her speaking.
           'What? All dumb
Conspirators? Now is your time. Now come,
You searchers of the truth, you diggers up
Of secrets, now come all of you, the cup†
Is full and brimming over and shall be poured   210
—You shall drink now. What? You—or you, my lord,
Forbid my wandering nights? Are you content
To lose your own? Will you, my lord, be pent
A prisoner every night within the wall,
You, General? Does one fetter bind us all?'
'Content?' he growled, 'Why, Madam, who that's sane
And 's slept in starlight many a long campaign,
Would leave his bed by nights? What should I seek

* moment
† Of secrets, *ask your fill. Come all,* the cup

[137]

Beyond my pillow, then?'—'Aye, Thus you speak,
Thus now you speak,' she said, 'When woods put on   220
Their daytime stillness, when the voice is gone
From rivers, and the cats of night lie curled
In sleep, and the moon moves beneath the world.
Fie! As if all that hear you did not know
The password, as yourself. Five hours ago
Where were you?—and with whom?—how far away?
Borrowing what wings of speed when break of day
Recalled you, to be ready, here, to rise
In the nick of time, and with your formal eyes
And grave talk, to belie that other face   230
And voice you've shown us in a different place?
What, mum as ever? Does the waking voice
So scare you on that theme? It is your choice
Not mine, to grub and drag the secret thence,
Where I've played fair . . . tho', faith, your long pretence
Has been my wonder: how you could return
Each morning to the mask and take concern,
Or seem to take concern, with toys—who's dead,
Who's suit is gone awry and whose is sped,
Who's beautiful, and who grows past her prime—   240
As if it were there your heart lay! All the time
That flame to which your waking hours are ash,
Shining so near . . . one syllable too rash,
One glance unveiled, had let the secret out;
But always you slipped past and went about,
Skilfully—like conspirators who meet
Out of their lodge, and pass, and do not greet.
Oh fools! . . . if all the plotting brethren turn
Informers against one, shall that one burn
Or hang defenceless? All to keep his vow   250
Of silence? I have a tongue, and freedom now
To use it. The pact's off. I'll force you yet
To throw down all the cards: and where we met,
By night, and what we were, you shall recall.
Tho' limp as a dead man's your tongues should crawl

[138]

Unwilling to the word,—I'll make them speak,
Up, from your graves! You're shamming. You shall shriek
To split the clouds with truth, you shall proclaim
On housetops what your muttering dared not name
In corners. Or, as Lazarus' ghost, beneath   260
The cloths, back to its shrunk and emptied sheath
Wormed its way home, I'll force again to grow,
Under these masks you wear for daylight show,
The selves you are at night . . .
                              What? Nothing yet?
No answer? . . . can it be you do forget?
Did the gates shut so quickly? Could you not bear
One small grain back to light and upper air?
Must I go down like Orpheus and retrace
The interdicted ford—out of that place,   270
Step by step, hand in hand, hale up what lies
Buried in you, and teach your waking eyes
To acknowledge it? I thought we had all known
What spends us in the dark, and why we groan
To feel the light return and the limbs ache,
Even in our slumber fighting not to wake . . .
I thought that you, being but the husks of men
All the drab day, remembered where and when
The ripe ear grows—where are the golden hills
It waves on, and the granaries it fills.   280
Call it again. Dive for it. Strain your sight,
Crack all your sinews, heaving up to light
What's under you. Thou sunken wreck, arise!,
Sea-gold, sea-gems that fill the hollow eyes
Of admirals dead; out of thy smothering caves
Where colour is not, up, to where the waves
Turn emerald and the edge of ocean-cold
Is yielding,* and the fish go slashed with gold,
Up!, 'gainst thy nature, up!, put on again
Colour and form and be to waking men   290
Things visible. Heave all! Softly . . . it rears

* breaking

[139]

Its dripping head. What, Lords? At last? Your ears
Remember now that song, those giant words,
Louder than woods that thundered, scattering birds
Like leaves along the sky, and whose the throats
Louder than cedars there whipt flat as oats . . .
Birds tumbled . . . the sky dipped . . .'
                                        The Queen's voice broke.
Heavily, in that moment, like the stroke
Of an axe* falling, came the sight and sense   300
Of those about her: the long room, packed dense,
Her voice yet stirring echoes in the corners,
Dull, puzzled eyes, the patient smile of scorners,
Face behind unintelligible face,
Arms nudging and heads whispering in each place
Save where she looked. Then twice she made endeavour,
Grasped the great moment's virtue: gone forever:
Struggling to speak. Then (curses on the frame
Of woman!) her breast shook, and scalding came
Tears of deep rage. Bit thro' the lip, clench hand,   310
—All's vain. And now she saw the Archbishop stand
Beside her, whispering, 'Daughter . . . come away.'
Heard the King's voice, 'The Queen's not well† to-day.'

* a sword
† Queen is sick

[140]

CANTO II

They dine at ten to three* in Drum;
At four the full decanters come
And, heavy with dark liquor, pass
Down the long tables polished smooth as glass,
In dark red rooms where the piled curtains sweep
Wine-coloured carpets ankle deep.
(Outside, the thrush sings: unobserved, the flowers
Drop petals through those silent† hours).
    The King, too tired to drink his wine in state,
Was with the Chancellor *tête-à-tête*.   10
The Chancellor who with punctual sip
Raised his full glass to bloodless lip
A moment later than his master
In perfect time, now slow, now faster.
The tiptoe servants from the room
Stole reverently as from a tomb;
The door closed softly as the settling wing
Of pigeons in a wood. The King
Threw off his wig and wiped his glistening head
And, 'Where's she now?' he said.   20

'The Queen, Sir? Since we left the Council board
I think she's mewed up somewhere with my lord
Archbishop.'

       'With old Daddy? Likely enough . . .
Do you suppose, now, he believes that stuff?'

* half-past two
† that pause of

[141]

'Daddy believe her? Oh Lord, Sir, not he!
Least of us all, Sir; less than you and me.'

'Why, as for that—fill up, fill both the glasses.
Steenie, your health! you understand . . . what passes
Between us—mum's the word. We two together   30
Have come through many a storm and change of weather.
In confidence, now; tell me what you made
This morning of our loving wife's tirade?'

'Me, Sir? I think the Queen . . . has startled Drum
Excessively. She'll have her following; some
Will doubtless—'

                    'I'm not asking what she'll do
To others, man, but what she's done to you.
Your glass is empty.'

                    'Well Sir, if you must.   40
Thank you. No more! Your Majesty . . . I trust
I may be pardoned if I hesitate;
The failure of our plan . . . the whole debate
Turned upside down . . . has thrown me in such doubt,
I looked to your advice to lead us out.'

'At least, you haven't passed it with a sneer
Like Daddy. You perceive there's . . . something . . . here?'

'Oh, not like Daddy, Sir. I'm humbler far.
These churchmen, in the bulk—'

                    'Why, there you are!   50
That's what I say. For if there were such things,
Some secret stairs and undiscovered wings
In the world's house, dark vacancies between
The rooms we know—behind the public scene
Some inner stage . . . if such things could be so,

[142]

The man who wears a mitre's paid to know
Or to invent it, eh? Of all men living
He's the least right to pass without misgiving.'

'Oh very true. I see, Sir. After all,
We might in sleep be more than we recall   60
On waking?'

       'Easy enough to talk at large
And laugh at her: but who'll refute the charge?
Like a puffed candle-flame at half past ten
My world goes out: at nine, perhaps, again
I find it . . .'

       'Yes indeed. And in between
No one can tell us where or what we've been.'

'Ah! There's the stickler, eh? We understand,
You and I, Steenie. Fill your glass. Your hand!   70
We don't remember.' ·

       'Yet . . . there's times, at waking,
One feels one has just failed in overtaking
Something . . . you can't say what . . . already, as your eyes
First catch it, shuffling on its day's disguise.'

'I know, Steenie. Like on the hills, if one
White cotton-tail has flashed, the mischief's done;
Where you saw nothing, now you see the ground
Alive with rabbits half a mile around,
And all betrayed by one. So one queer thought   80
Peeps from the edge of sleep, and there you've caught
The implication of a thousand others,
And then . . . you're wide awake. Common sense smothers
The trail of the fugitives.'

       'But if one delves
As deep as that . . .'

'Speak out: only ourselves
Will hear you.'

                'Why . . . your Majesty has such a way!
I'm in an odd, confessing mood to-day.   90
I hardly know . . . it's strange we've never spoken
Of things like that . . . he-he! . . . I think the Queen has broken
Our dams all down—'

            'What's that?'

                             'I said, the Queen
Had opened all the doors: that is, I mean—'

'That wasn't what you said.'

                      'I said, the Queen
Had broken in the dams.'

                  'Oh, very good!   100
Excellent . . . dykes in Holland . . . and the flood,
Disnatured for a hundred years, sighs-off the chain,
Easing its heart, and floods the land again.
I'll tell you what I feel . . . I think I know
How it would feel to be a man of snow
Set in the sunlight . . . yes: that's how I feel—
Deliciously soft liquefactions steal
Round the stiff corselet where we've frozen in
The fluid soul, so long . . . and drops begin
To hollow out warm caves and paths . . . but you,   110
You said, if one delved deep—?'

                    'Why, if you do,
Well, frankly—in such glances—well, by God!
I've fished up things that were extremely odd.'

'I know the kind (come, drink about) and Daddy
Had reasons to ignore it.'

                  [144]

'Reasons, had he?
You mean he knows?'

　　　　　'He guesses well enough
That back there on the borderland there's stuff　　　120
Not marked on any map their sermons show
—They keep one eye shut just because they know—
Don't we all know?
At bottom?—that this World in which we draw
Our salaries, make our bows, and keep the law,
This legible, plain universe we use
For waking business, is a thing men choose
By leaving out . . . well, much; our editing,
(With expurgations) of some larger thing?
Well, then, it stands to reason; go behind　　　130
To the archetypal scrawl, and there you'll find
. . . Well . . . variant readings, eh? And it won't do
Being over-dainty there.'

　　　　　'That's very true.
Can't wear kid gloves.'

　　　　　'Once in a way, perhaps,
's pardonable—wholesome even—to relapse.
You never feel it, yet this keeping hold
Year after year . . . eh? . . . that's what makes us old.
Now when one was a boy . . . do you remember　　　140
(You'd have been twelve that year) one warm September
Under those laurels, with the keeper's dog
And the gypsy girl—the day we killed the frog?'

'Boys will be boys, Sir! By your leave again,
I'll fill your glass and mine. But now we're men
How can you reach . . . how does the Queen contrive
To keep the memory of her nights alive
Though we've forgotten?'

　　　　　'Why—plague on her—she
Goes thither in the body.'　　　150

[145]

'Didn't we?
I put a bold face on while she was making
Her speech this morning: but a knee-cap aching
And a bruised shin kept running in my head.
The devil!—how should knees get knocks in bed?'

'That's sympathetic magic . . . like Saint Francis . . .
Stigmata . . . when the Subtle Body dances
Ten miles away, you feel the palpitations.
. . . Like the wax doll for witches' incantations.
That fortune-telling man they whipped and branded.   160
What was his name?'

                    'Oh he was caught red-handed.
The floating lady and the flying tambourine . . .
All done by wires, Sir, Jesseran* you mean?
Why, if he's still alive, he's down below
Under the castle here. They loved him so
The people, and believed him; he was tried
In secret. But beyond all doubt he's died.
It's down to water level, under clay,
The dungeons of your father's father's day—   170
No one could live. The keepers hardly know
The way down; and it's twenty years ago.'

'I'll dig him up, though. For our present game,
Living or dead, he might be much the same.
What?—never stare. I thought you understood.
Help me up, Steenie. So! I'm in the mood
For a frolic. Are those dams all down? Oh brave!
Trol-de-rol-trol! The emalgipated slave . . .
Wouldn't a lobster, now, feel more than well
If some kind friend unbuttoned 'm from 's shell!   180
That's how I feel. Hey, Steenie, watch your legs.
Let's have a song.'
                    * Gesseran

[146]

'This way, Sir. 'Ware the table.
I hold it, Sir, most seriously,
Both treasonous and treasonable,
Privatus homo, subjects such as me,
When Majesty is drunk, in contrariety
To flaunt an illegalical sobriety.'

'Excellent! Have that in the statute book.
Steenie . . . my old, old friend . . . how beautiful you look.   190
We'll go to the dungeons, eh?'

                        'Absolutely deeper.
To the centre of the earth. We'll wake the sleeper.
Trumpets there!'

                    'We'll sing charms and ride on brooms
We'll fetch the dead men out of tombs,
We'll get with child the mountain hags
And ride the cruels of the crags . . .
How gardens love it when the gardener's eye
's wi'drawn a month, and ten feet high   200
The weeds foam round the cottage door . . .
Their dykes are down . . . the tide returns once more.
Liberty! Liberty! as the duchess says
Each night when they undo her stays.
Remember how the iambic goes?
Ἐπιλελήσμεθ᾽ ἡδέως.*
Open the door there! Both! The other wing!
My lordge—The King is drunk; long live the King!'

                    *Transl.: 'We forget sweetly.'

[147]

CANTO III

The dungeon stair interminably round and round
Draws on the King and Chancellor far underground
To his ancestral prison-house. And in the tower
The Queen and the Archbishop in her airy bower
Sit talking; the frail, slender tower that overlooks
Meadows and wheeling windmills and meandering brooks
Five miles towards the mountains of the spacious west.
The mountains swell towards them like a woman's breast,
Their winding valleys, bountiful like opened hands,
Spread out their green embracement to the lower lands,   10
The pines on the peak'd ridges, like the level hair
Of racing nymphs are stretched on the clear western air.
Often she looked towards them and her eyes were brightened,
And her pulse quickened, her brow lightened;
And often at the old man's voice she turned her head,
And each time more impatiently. 'My lord', she said,
'If you had laughed me down like all the rest,
I would have understood. But you've confessed
Such things may be. Then what we both believe
You'd keep a secret?'—'Lest I should deceive,'   20
Said he, 'I hold my tongue. Truths may be such
That when they have cooled and hardened at the touch
Of language, they turn errors. So our speech
Fails us, and waking discourse cannot reach
The thing we are in dreams. Alas, my Queen,
What Spirit, while nature sleeps, has done or seen,
If told at morning, fades like fairy wealth,
And in its place the changeling comes by stealth,
The dapper lie, more marketable far
Than truth, the maid. Daughter, I think you are   30

[148]

Willingly no deceiver. What you meant
To-day was truth; but all that truth was spent
Before you said ten words. What followed after
—All the wild tale you told of storm and laughter
And hunting on the hills—all this . . . (good now
On your salvation, never change your brow,
Soft! Softly! Quench those eyes)
All this, by a plain word, was it not lies?'

'How lies my lord, when all the talk of Drum
Vouches my wanderings real? Play fairly. Come!   40
That I've gone there, is known; that I've met you
When you were also there, is that not true?'

'Have I been in that place? (We'll call it so
Though wrongly) . . . have I? . . . child, I do not know.
Sometimes I think I have. I am uncertain.
Ask me not. If a man could lift the curtain
The half-inch that's beyond all price—but none
Can tell, being wakened, what the night has done.'

Her scorn leaped quickly at him. 'If you know
Thus little of the lands to which I go,   50
How can you call my tale of them untrue?
Give me the lie who can! so cannot you.'

'This is but baby's talk,' he said, 'Indeed
We cannot lift the curtain at our need,
It is immovable, but lights come through.
We know not—we remember that we knew.'
And then he paused, and ruefully he smiled
Fondling his knee with thoughful hand; and, 'Child,'
He said, 'How can it profit us to talk
Much of that region where you say you walk.   60
We are not native there: we shall not die
Nor live in elfin country, you and I.
Greatly I fear lest, wilfully refusing

[149]

Beauty at hand, you walk dark roads to find it,
Impatient of dear earth because behind it
You dream of phantom worlds, forever losing
What is more wonderful—too strange indeed
For you—too dry a flavour for the greed
Of uncorrected palates; this sweet form
Of day and night, the stillness and the storm,   70
Children, the changing year, the growing god
That springs, by labour, out of the turn'd sod.'

'I have no child,' she said, 'What mockery is this,
What jailor's pittance offered in the prison of earth,
To that unbounded appetite for larger* bliss
Not born with me, but older than my mortal birth? . . .
When shall I be at home? When shall I find my rest?
My lord, you have lived happy and with cause have blessed
This world's habitual highway, where you walk at ease;
I walk not, but go naked upon bleeding knees.   80
And if this threadbare vanity of days, this lean
And never-ceasing world were all—if I must lose
The air that breathes across it from the land I've seen,
About my neck tonight I'd slip the noose
And end the longing. But it is not so;
And you—your words have half revealed—you know,
And will not tell. Oh pity, pity I crave
(This thirst will burn my body in the rotting grave)
Speak to me, father! tell me all the truth, confess!
Give me a plain No or an honest Yes.   90
Have you too found the way to such a place,
And in it have we all met face to face?'

'Peace, peace! Beware!'

                    'Of what should I beware?
What is the crucifixion that I would not dare,
To find my home? (When shall my rest be won?)
Why do you turn away: What have I done?'

                    * longer

[150]

'Almost crushed dead, I fear, on your own breast
With hot, rough, greedy hands what you love best.
It will not thus be wooed. You will not find   100
Your rest while such a storm is in your mind—
You may find something else.'

                    'What do you mean?'

'Listen: there are two sorts of the unseen,
Two countries each from each removed as far
As the black dungeons of this castle are
From this green mountain and this golden sun.
And of the first, I say, we do not know;
But the other is beneath, where to and fro
Through echoing vaults continually chaos vast   110
Works in the cellarage of the soul, and things exiled,
And foolish giants howling from the ancestral past
Wander, and overweening Hopes, and Fears too wild
For this slow-ripening universe; chimeras, ghosts,
And succubi and cruelties. You are* more like,
Driven on by such a fury of desire, to strike
Those rocks than to make harbour on the happy coasts.
Wishing is perilous work.'

                    'Go on', she said.
'What more?' the Bishop asked, and turned his head   120
Slowly away; 'What more is there to tell?'

'You have described the downward journey well,
But of the realm of light, have you no word?'

'Nothing but that which all mankind have heard.'

She turned away, she paced the floor,
She waited for the Bishop's word no more.
And he looked down, and more than once he passed
His hand across his face, and then at last

                    * and

[151]

Spoke gently, as a man in much distress.
'Daughter,' he said, 'I see I must confess.   130
God knows I am an old, fat, sleek divine
—Lived easily all my life—far deeper skilled
In nice discriminations of old wine
Than in those things for which God's blood was spilled.
Enough of that. And now my punishment
Has found me and my time of grace is spent;
For now I must speak truth and find at need
My advocacy kills the cause I plead.
For if I say none knows, no man is sure
Of anything about that land, your eyes,   140
Seeing me thus world-ridden, thus impure,
How can they, if they would, judge otherwise
Than that my disallegiance from the laws
Of Spirit has dulled my edge and been the cause
Of this great ignorance I profess? How, then,
Believe me when I teach that holiest men
Are not less ignorant? (So I think, but I—
What do I know of saints or sanctity?)
But so I think; and so perforce I come
Into the court, though shamed, not daring to be dumb.   150
Hear, then, my tale.
I, who stand ignorant confessed,
Doctor of nescience, or, at best,
A plodding passman in the school
Meek Wonder and her maidens rule,
Who hold the brave world's blue and green
But for a magic-lantern screen
That enigmatically shows
The shadow of what no one knows;—
I yet believe (if such a word   160
Of these soiled lips be not absurd)
That from the place beyond all ken
One only Word has come to men,
And was incarnate and had hands
And feet and walked in earthly lands

[152]

And died, and rose. And nothing more
Will come or ever came before
With certainty. And to obey
Is better than the hard assay
Of piercing anywhere besides   170
This mortal veil, which haply hides
Some insupportable abyss
Of bodiless light and burning bliss.
Hence, if you ask me of the way
Yonder, what can I do but say
Over again (as God's own Son
Seems principally to have done)
The lessons of your nurse and mother?
For all my counsel is no other
Than this, now given at bitterest need;   180
—Go, learn your catechism and creed.
Mark what I say, not how I live,
And for myself—may God forgive.'

'I thought as much,' she cried. 'That pale,
Numbing, inevitable tale,
The deathbed of desire! Why do you cease?
Preach out your sermon, tell me now of peace
Of passions calmed with grey renunciation,
Longsuffering and obedience and salvation!
What is all this to me? Where is my home   190
Save where the immortals in their exultation,
Moon-led, their holy hills forever roam?
What is to me your sanctity, grave-clothed in white,
Cold as an altar, pale as altar candle light?
Not to such purpose was the plucking at my heart
Wherever beauty called me into lonely places,
Where dark Remembrance haunts me with eternal smart,
Remembrance, the unmerciful, the well of love,
Recalling the far dances, the far-distant faces,
Whispering me 'What does this—and this—remind you of?'   200
How can I cease from knocking or forget to watch—'

[153]

But other fingers now were on the latch
And with a swaggering stride a noisy, thin,
Hurried, portentous person had come in.
'Madam,' he squeaked, 'I've come to let you know
The Leader calls for both of you below.'
Anger so stopped her heart and held her eyes
That, staring hard, she could not recognise
That pale face twisted with the uneasy thirst
Of looking more than even now it durst,   210
Hinting the tavern glance *en mousquetaire*
Yet flinching, too, beneath her silent stare.
At last she knew—the ill-mannered boy, the same
Who at the council had bemired her name,
And at the door behind him she could see
Men with fixed bayonets standing, two or three.
And then she laughed—unsummoned laughter, light
And careless from the immeasurable height
Of unflawed youth, and said 'What madness now?'
It was a world to see his reddening brow   220
And watch his venom'd fingers how they twist.
'Oh very fine! But that's all done,' he hissed.
'And I'm no more your very humble dog.
Trust me, my lady, we have killed King Log
Under whose reign the license of your tongue
Has ladied it and laughed at us so long.
We have a Leader now, and you've a master.
Don't ask me who! You'll learn the story faster
Than you desire, perhaps: and you'll have leisure
To learn your duties and the Leader's pleasure.   230
For it's a new world now—and back to Drum
The days of our great ancestors are come.
The seven isles will tremble to the core,
And Terebinthia, when we go to war.
You shall behold the Leader when he comes
Riding the foremost of a thousand chargers
All white as milk, a conqueror, home to Drum,
Laden with pearls of Tessaropolis

And gold of Galma,* while in silver chains
The Emperor of the East attends his state   240
And Kings enslaved and many a captive isle.
Oh brave to be a Duce! brave to drink
The melted pearls of Tessaropolis
And burn the towers of many a captive isle
And to be called a Duce . . . but, meanwhile,
For both of you the Leader waits below.'

And steel was at their backs. They had to go.
                    * Calma

CANTO IV

I

The Queen and the Archbishop and the Boy descend
Slowly by many stairways to the castle hall.
Often it seems a journey that will never end,
Often it seems a moment. They are silent all,
Thinking hard thoughts. The Bishop thinks them most of all.
    For the Queen has heard a trumpet in her heart, and smiles;
She is buckling on her byrnie every step they go,
Ready to die or ready to use all her wiles
—Fierce Artemis will help her. She has learned to know,
Long since, those pains and pleasures which the hunted know.   10
    But he thinks how his Christendom is all to learn,
His soul to set and harden in the mould that makes
Eternal spirit, his leprosy to heal and turn
Fresh as the skin of childhood, in the time it takes
To reach the hall. (Incalculable time it takes;
    The Watchers from beyond the world perceive each stair
Long with sidereal distances beyond all count,
A ladder of humility stretched up to where
The eternal forests tremble on the leavèd mount
Of Paradise. Up thither they behold him mount.)   20
    They reached the bottom of the bottom stair and passed
Into the hall. The General stood here, so vast,
With legs astride, so planted, that he seemed to bear
The weight of the whole house upon his shoulders square.
His red, full blood grandiloquently in his cheek
Spoke so that you could almost say his body shouted
And was his garish blazon ere his tongue could speak,
Saying, 'I am the leader, the event, the undoubted,

All-potent Fact, the firstborn of necessity,
I am Fate, and Force, and Führer, Worship me!'   30

II

The General at the council-board had heard
The Queen's harangue that day with scarce a word,
   Indifferent first, and then amused, and then
Something within him in response had stirred.

All those nocturnal wanderings must be
A girlish dream, he thought, undoubtedly,
   But if it came to dredging up one's dreams,
Well—he'd had curious nights as well as she.

He did not share the popular dismay.
No; if she wanted dreams to walk by day,   40
   He was her man—only remained to see
If his or hers would bear the greater sway.

Perhaps, indeed, no conflict would arise;
The General thought he had a shrewd surmise
   How hers would look when his experienced hand
Had eased them of their troublesome disguise.

For though this happened long before the name
Of Freud or his disciples rose to fame,
   Men like the General, even then, had reached
(Empirically) doctrines much the same.   50

When Council rose, about his work he went,
And warnings to his gunmen all he sent,
   And seized a press and moved some troops. He'd missed
His dinner, but the time had been well spent.

And so it came to pass, at five o'clock
The Jailor of the dungeons turned his lock
   To let the King and Chancellor in. And down,
Singing, they went into the tunnelled rock.

At five past, he was visited again
—This time the General and a dozen men.   60
   He clicked his heels. 'How many entrances,'
The General asked, 'lead down into that den?'

'Only this one, your honour,' he replied.
'Good!' said the General, plucking from his side
   His bunch of keys. And to his men, 'Now boys,'
He said. They kicked the Jailor down inside.

They slammed and locked the door and turned away.
Inside, the Jailor heard the General say
   'The keys? Oh throw them in the well. The fools
Chose to go down. I choose that they can stay.'   70

And soon the castle was extremely still,
For all were killed whom they proposed to kill.
   Servants with ashen face and hair on end
Came scampering at a call to do his will.

He said he liked his victuals with some taste;
He'd have a two-pint jug of porter, laced
   With brandy, hot as hell, and devilled bones
And good strong cheese. And it was brought in haste.

He shovelled all these things inside his head,
And smacked his lips (large lips, and moist and red),   80
   And belched a little, tapping with his whip
His booted calves. 'Now for the girl!' he said.

The Bishop and the Queen arrived. He said,
'Madam, the King is both deposed and dead.
The Why and Wherefore of it's long to hear,
And politics are not a woman's sphere.
The King is dead—and your bereavement such
As you can bear without lamenting much
. . . Why! it's mere nature. If I made pretence
Of sympathy, it would insult your sense,
Aye, and your senses too—which never yet
Had anything from him you need regret.
Now listen—for you're neither prude nor dunce
And I can tell you my whole mind at once;
First, let me make it absolutely clear
That nobody has anything to fear
From me—provided that I get my way.
I'm always nice to people who obey,
Specially girls: and if you are kind to me
I will repay it double. Try! and see
How much more rich, more splendid and more gay
Your court will be than in the old King's day.
As for myself, I am not young, it's true,
At least, my dear, not quite so young as you;
But young at heart—and our blunt soldiers say
Old fiddles often are the best to play.
I'm not a jealous man: I'll leave you free
Except in one thing only. There must be
No more night wanderings nor no talk of them:
All that I most explicitly condemn . . .
It's nonsense too. Henceforth you must confine
Your limbs to bed o'nights—and that bed mine!'

No one could feel the quick of the Queen's heart
Except the Queen, and she had learned her part.
Just long enough she cast her look aside

90

100

110

And fluttered, then with silver voice replied,
'As for our consort, doubtless soon or late
The elderly must pay their debts to fate,
And young wives are aware they must submit
To widowhood—indeed they count on it.
Enough: the future is our chief concern.   120
Surely your Lordship has not now to learn
That his heroic deeds are eloquence
In female ears, admitting no defence.
In all ways irresistible you come,
Conqueror of things unconquered yet in Drum!
If I should play the girl and hang my head,
It would but show me rustic and ill-bred;
Yet, if I might demur, this time and place
Are hardly suitable in such a case.   130
These your heroic followers;—I am proud
To welcome them—but still, they make a crowd,
Nor can my answer be so full and clear
As your high dignity deserves—not here.
In Paphos, Sir, not midst the watchful stars
Of public heaven, does Venus welcome Mars;
And, by your leave withdrawn into my tower,
I will await the Leader's private hour.'

'Come!' said the General, 'That's the sort of stuff!
Perhaps my methods were a trifle rough.
I am a plain, blunt soldier, as no doubt   140
You saw: but you have kindly helped me out.
Go to your tower, and I'll be there at six
But (in your ear, my lady) play no tricks!
Women are changeable! eh? no offence
But you shall have an escort with you hence.
Here! You!' (He called the raw-boned boy, whose name
I cannot give, for it is lost to fame)
'Go, follow to her bower the Queen of Drum,
And keep your eye upon her till I come.   150
If she escapes, you'd better face the devil

Than me: but if she finds you are uncivil,
By heaven I'll make you the first precedent
For eunuchs in my court. Now go!'

They went.

IV

The Leader takes a turn and rubs his hands,
Chuckling and murmuring 'Who'd have thought it now?'
And then he comes where the Archbishop stands
And pulls the old man to him by the sleeve
Into a window, with a graver brow   160
Politically furrowed. 'I believe
We know each other pretty well,' said he,
'Experienced people seldom disagree.
You see there's been a change. I'm called to fill
The supreme office, by the people's will
Or, strictly, what the people will discover
To have been their will when all the shouting's over.
Now, in this new regime, of course your Grace
Must certainly retain his present place
And power and temporalities. Indeed,   170
If I might criticise, we rather need
Not less but more of what you represent;
For up till now—pray, take this as it's meant,
Kindly—a certain somnolence has come
To be the hall mark of the Church of Drum,
For several years. Henceforward that won't do;
And naturally I rely on you.
Faith—martyrdom—and all that side of things
Concerns Dictators even more than Kings.
Can you contrive a really hot revival,   180
A state religion that allows no rival?
You understand, henceforth it's got to be

A Drummian kind of Christianity—
A good old Drummian god who has always some
Peculiar purpose up His sleeve for Drum,
Something that makes the increase of our trade
And territories feel like a Crusade,
Or, even if neither should in fact increase,
Teaches men in my will to find their peace.
Those are the general principles. But now   190
The problem is (and you must show me how)
To deal with the late sovereign's disappearance.
I doubt if they'd believe in interference
From Heaven direct—a plain, Old Testament
Annihilation on the tyrant sent . . .
But, short of that, we either must produce
The corpse, or else some plausible excuse.
What do you think? The matter's in your line
And suited to your office more than mine.'

The Bishop answered, 'Any man in the world   200
Has more right to rebuke these words than I.
But I believe—I know you could not know
That I believed—in God. I dare not lie.'

The General answered, 'I should hope you do;
I'm a religious man as well as you,
But now we're talking politics. You say
That you believe; the point is, so do they,
Which makes all doctrines easy to digest.
Come, now; I've made a very small request.'

'I cannot tell them more than I believe.
I dare not play with such immeasurables.
I am afraid: yes, that's the truth, afraid,
Put it no higher. Fear would stop my tongue.'

The Leader said, 'Oh Lord, to have a fool
To deal with. God Almighty, keep me cool!

[162]

What do you fear? Have I not made it plain,
You and your Church have everything to gain?
Be loyal to the Leader and I'll build
Cathedrals for you, yes, and see them filled,
I'll give you a free hand to bait all Jews   220
And infidels. You can't mean to refuse?'

'I must: for He of whom I am afraid
Esteems the gifts that [you] can promise me
Evil, or else of very small account.'

'Silence!' The Leader said, 'Silence, I say!
You never talked like this before to-day,
And now to make religion your pretence,
Frankly, I hold it sheer irreverence.
If you look down from such a starry height
As that, upon all earthly power and might,   230
Why, in God's name, have you not told us so
A year, or ten, or fifteen years ago?
Why was your other-worldliness so dumb
When every office went for sale in Drum,
When half the people had no bread to eat
Because the Chancellor'd cornered* all the wheat,
When the Queen played her witchery nights, and when
The old King had his women nine or ten?
All this you saw, unless you were asleep.
God! to sit still beside the course and keep   240
Your malice hid, till at the race's end
You dart your leg out to trip up a friend
Just at the goal. I'd counted upon you—
The thing so dangerous and my friends so few,
Would I have risked it if I thought the Church
Was going to turn and leave me in the lurch?
What? Silent still? Why then, damnation take you!
I've begged enough, I'll find a way to make you.
You've played a dirty trick, and now you'll rue it!'
He called his men and said, 'Boys! Put him through it.'   250

* corner

[163]

V

The raw-boned boy, meanwhile, was with the Queen.
She led him in the short way between
The great hall and her private tower,
—A little terrace, at that hour
A solitary place. And there
She knew that they would pass a stair
Down which she had scampered many a night
Into the garden by star-light.
Upon her arm she had a ring,
The bridal gift of the old King,   260
Hard, heavy gold that twists to take
The likeness of a tangled snake.
She works it downwards as they walk,
Little she heeds her jailor's talk.
She works it till that golden worm
Is round her knuckles and held firm.
And now they reached the stairway's head.
Never a word the lady said;
Out from her shoulder straight she flung
Her arm, so strong, so round, so young;   270
His wits were much too slow to save him—
It was a lovely blow she gave him.

Right in his mouth with all her strength
He got the gold. He sprawled his length,
Bloodied and blubbering; and when
He scrambled to his feet again,
He saw the wide, smooth lawn between
Himself and the swift-footed queen,
He saw her raiment flickering white
Against the hedge—then out of sight.   280

VI

The Leader's ruffians gather with great strokes
About the Bishop, with lead pipe and sticks,

As foresters about a tree with the axe,
With belts and bludgeons and with jibes and jokes.
His breath comes grunting under heavy shocks,
He pants so loud, they think that he still talks,
And rail upon him crying Plague and Pox!
Ever a bone breaks or a sinew cracks.
They beat upon his stomach till its wall breaks.   Aoi!

In his imagination he seems to hang   290
Upon a cross and be tormented long,
Not nailed but gripping with his fingers strong.
With the toil thereof all his muscles are wrung,
Great pains he bears in shoulder, arm and lung.
He fears lest they should jolt the cross and fling
His body off from where he has to hang.   Aoi!

Ever he calls to Christ to be forgiven
And to come soon into the happy haven.
Horrible dance before his eyes is woven
Of darkened shapes on a red tempest driven.   300
Unwearyingly the great strokes are given.
He falls. His sides and all his ribs are riven,
His guts are scattered and his skull is cloven,
The man is dead. God has his soul to heaven.   Aoi!

CANTO V

Wing'd with delight and fear, the Queen
Was running on the ridgy green.*
Up the first field that gently slopes
Towards the hills of all her hopes,
Happy the man who might have seen
The unripe breasts of that young Queen
So panting, and her face above
So flushed and eye-bright for his love,
As in this unregarding place
She breathed, she brightened, with the chase.   10
Up the long field in open view
Only to get her lead she flew,
But in the next she hugged the edge
Well hidden by the blackthorn hedge,
Then through the spinney chose a track
Still up, not daring to look back,
Then forty yards of sunken lane
Up hill, then to her left again,
Half level, and half losing ground
—For so she must to sidle round   20
A big ten-acre field where men
Were still at work, though even then
Looking with welcome in their eyes
To the slow-yellowing† western skies.
It was the hour when grass looks greener
And hay smells sweeter. None had seen her,
When up beyond the fields she came

* *These two lines originally followed lines 3 and 4*
† slow-brightening

[166]

Where three parts wild and one part tame
Old horses roll and donkeys bray
And geese in choleric cohorts stray   30
About the common land, that now
Springs steeply to the foot-hill's brow.
Here as she breasted the hot track
Baked with the sun, she first looks back
And sees the squat-built castle stand
Spider-like amid smooth Drum-land,
And from it, spreading like a fan,
The hunt she fled from—horse and man
Already dark and dwarf'd as ants
But creeping, nearing. While she pants,   40
Hard labouring up the stony ground
And slippery grass, above the sound
Of her blood hammering in her ears,
Music of baying dogs she hears.
Her wind is good, her feet are fast,
She knows how long they both will last,
On hounds and horses she has reckoned.
She gains that crest, and towards the second
Swifter she runs, yet not too swift.
Here the whole earth begins to lift   50
Its large limbs under robes of green
Higher, and deepening gaps between
Sink in warm shadow, and the sky,
Jostled with peaks, shows small and high.
The land of Drum is seen no longer,
The world is purer, the light stronger
And streams and falls and everywhere
More streams sound on the quiet air.
    Here well she knew her way, to turn
And find an amber-coloured burn   60
That musical with myriad shocks
Of water leaped its stair of rocks:
And up the stream from hold to hold
She clambered—the knife-edge of cold

Deliciously now reached her waist,
Now splashed her lips with earthen taste,*
There wading, leaping in and out
She climbed to throw the trail in doubt,
And reached the head. High moorland lay
Before her, and peaks far away
And over them the broad sun sinking.

She stood to breathe a moment, thinking
Of many small things, many a place
Far from that evening's toil and chase,
Until the bloodhounds' noise behind
Came louder on a change of wind,
And quelled her spirit as she hearkened,
And drove her on.

The world was darkened.†

And still she runs, but slowly now, and yet
More slowly, and pain burns her feet, and sweat
Tangles her hair on smarting eyes and brow;
And still she runs; only of running now
She thinks, not of the ending of the chase,
But always runs. There is a wretched place

*. . . earthen taste,

> And now on the rock slabs her feet
> Touch dry, warm moss and found it sweet.
> There wading . . .

†. . . was darkened.

> Peak after peak, that had stood single
> Stole from her tired eyes to mingle
> And melt its fluid shape among
> The notch-edged darkness whence it sprung;
> And all one gloom the moorland grew
> Save where some pool had caught the hue
> Of the sky's deepening arch that spread
> Pale and enormous overhead.

> And still . . .

Beyond the moor, right underneath the fells,
The last of homesteads, where a miser dwells—
A huddle of trees, a cottage under thatch,
A meadow and a cultivated patch.
Often in her night wanderings before   90
She had seen old Trap, and often from his door
He had shouted at her shadow 'Witch!' and 'Whore!'
Thither she ran and entered the low wood,
Sure-footed, silent as a beast pursued,
And from the covert, shaping both her lips
A way she knew, pressed with her finger tips,
Sent such a cry that no man in the dark
But would have sworn it was a vixen's bark.
It worked! Old Trap had poultry to defend;
That eldritch sound had hardly time to end   100
Before the miser with his gun was out
To shoot the varmint dead. But round about
The shadowy Queen had gone to his back door,
Lifted the latch and trod on his cool floor,
And in a trice his pan of creaming milk
Down her dry throat went travelling smooth as silk;
Two apples and a lump of his goat cheese
She snatched,* and laughed, and under darkening trees
Stole on—now let him guess what nightly fairy
Or catamountain has enjoyed his dairy!   110
And up his meadow grass she glided,
The last green place before the world of rocks,
And all the lives of darkness sided
With her: the veritable fox
Welcomed with joy his hunted sister,
The small things of the ditches bade her
Good fortune, glad that man had missed her,
The mountains spread their slopes to aid her;
The world was changing: night was waking
And mountain silence, all-estranging.   120
Now as she ran she saw the meadow

*took

[169]

Darkened before her with her shadow,
Because the moon grew strong.* She turned;
Brittle and bright the crescent burned,
The thin and honey-coloured bow
Of the pure Huntress riding low.
Then to that sight her arm she raised,
Asking no favour, while she praised
The queen whose shafts destroy and bless
All wild souls of the wilderness,
Dark Hecate, Diana chaste,   130
Virginal dread of woods and waste,
Titania, shadowy fear and bliss
Of elf-spun night, great Artemis.
Deep her idolatry, for all,
Body and soul, beyond recall
She offered there: and body soon
Was filled all through with virtue of the moon,
That, like a spirit, in each tender vein
Flowed with nepenthe's power and eased all pain,   140
All weariness; and faster now she ran
Than when the toilsome chase began,
If it were running, for she seemed to glide
Over rough scree and rocky shelf
Smooth as a floating ship, through wide
And silvery lakes, or (like the moon herself,
Lapped in a motion which is also rest)—
To see the pale world's moonlit vest
Flit past beneath her—glimmering rocks
And tufts of grass like snowy locks,   150
Rivers of mercury, and towers
Of ebony, and stones like flowers.
Far over the piled hills, and past
The hills she knew, she travelled fast;
She found a valley like a cup
With moonshine to the brim filled up,
So pure a sweep of hollow ground,

*had risen] grew bright

[170]

Treeless, with turf so short around,
That not one shadow there could fall
But, smooth like liquid, over all,
Night's ghastly parody of day,
The lidless stare of moonlight lay.
Down into it, and straight ahead,
A single path before her led,
—A mossy way; and two ways more
There met it on the valley floor;
From left and right they came, and right
And left ran on out of the light.
And near that parting of three ways
She thought there was a silver haze,
She thought there was a giant's head
Pushed from the earth with whiteness spread
Of beard beneath and from its crown
Cataracts of whiteness tumbling down.
Then she drew near, tip-toed in awe,
And looked again; this time she saw
It was a thornbush, milky white
That poured sweet smell upon the night.
And nearer yet she came and then,
Bathed in its fragrance, looked again,
And lo! it was a horse and rider,
Breathing, unmoving, close beside her
More beautiful and larger
Than earthly beast, that charger,
Where rode the proudest rider;
—Rich his arms, bewitching
His air—a wilful, elfin
Emperor, proud of temper,
In mail of eldest moulding*
And sword of elven silver,
Smiling to beguile her;

* ... moulding

                         And milkwhite cloak of silkworm
                         And sword ...

160

170

1

A pale king, come from the unwintered country
Bending to her, befriending her, and offering white
Sweet bread like dew, his handsel at that region's entry,
And honey pale as gold is in the moonlit night.
When his lips opened, poignant as the unripened note
Of early thrush at evening was his words' deceiving,
The first few notes a-roving, then a silver rush.
'Keep, keep,' he bade her, 'On the midmost moss-way,
Seek past the cross-way to the land you long for.
Eat, eat,' he gave her of the loaves of faerie.   200
'Eat the brave honey of bees no man enslaveth.
Heed not the road upon the right—'twill lead you
To heaven's height and the yoke whence I have freed you;
Nor seek not to the left, that so you come not
Through the world's cleft into that world I name not.
Keep, keep the centre! Find the portals
That chosen mortals at the world's edge enter.
Isles untrampled by the warying legions
Of Heaven and Darkness—the unreckoned regions   210
That only as fable in His world appear
Who seals man's ear as much as He is able . . .
Many are the ancient mansions,
Isles His wars defile not,
Woods and land unwounding
The want whereof did haunt you;
Asked for long with anguish,
They open now past hoping
—All you craved, incarnate
Come like dream to Drum-land.'   220

Warm was the longing, warm as lover's laughter,
Strong, sweet, and stinging, that welled up to drift her
Away to the unwintry country, softer
Than clouds in clearest distance of Atlantic evening.
Warm was the longing; cold the dread
That entered after it. On her right hand

[172]

Descends* the insupportable. She turned her head,
But saw no more the air and moonlit land.
On all that side the world seemed falling,
From her own side the flesh seemed falling. 230
Dying, opening, melting, vanishing.
Yet to the sagging torment of that dissolution
She clung, contented with the vanishing
If only the fear'd moment never would arise
Of being commanded to lift up her eyes
And to see that whose dissimilitude
To all things should, in the first stare†
Of its aloofness,‡ make the world despair.
And that world was falling,
And her flesh was falling 240
And she was small; oh! were she small enough for crawling
Into some cranny under some small grass's root—
Rolled to a ball, dead-still beneath the Terror's foot;
To cover her face, close eyes, bury the closed eyes, and though
All hope to be unseen were madness, not to see,
Never to see, not to look up, never to know . . .
And all the world was falling
And her mind was falling.
Then, on a level with her own, there came
A face to which she could have given a name, 250
A face she had seen often (sinking down
Into foamed silvery beard and snowy gown),
And though it looked not as she thought the dead
Would look, she knew it spoke from among the dead,§

* It came,

† To all things, water, rocks, and air
      And sap-green lives and the warm blooded brood,
      With its aloofness should, in the first stare

‡ Unlikeness

§ . . . among the dead,
      A long way off. The small ancestral dread
      Mixed with the world's and with her soul's falling,
      Dread within dread. She heard it calling
      'Quick. . . .

'Quick. The last chance. Believe not the seducing elf.
Daughter, turn back, have pity yet upon yourself
Go not to the unwintering land where they who dwell
Pay each tenth year the tenth soul of their tribe to Hell.
Hear not the voice that promises, but rather hear
His who commands, and fear. We have all cause to fear. 260
Oh draw not down the* anger, which is far away
And slow to wake. Turn homeward ere the end of day.
You would not see if you looked up out of your torment
That face—only the fringes of His outer garment
Run to it, daughter; kiss that hem.' She answered, 'No.
If you are with Him pray to Him that He may go,
Or pray that He may rend and tear me,
But go, go hence and not be near me.'
And all the world was falling,
Spirit and soul were falling,
Body, brain and heart 270
Vanishing, falling apart;
Vacancy under vacancy
Shuddering gaped below;
'Go,' was her prayer, 'Go,
Go away, go away, away from me.'
And the fear heightened,
The command tautened;
Between her spirit and soul, dividing,
The razor-edged, ice-brook cold command was gliding, 280
Till suddenly, at the worst, all changed,
And like a thing far off, estranged,
Only remembered, like a mood,
That dread became. Her mortal blood
Flowed freely in the uncoloured calm,
Which woos† despair and is its balm.
Nothing now she will ever want again
But to glide out of all the world of men,
Nor will she turn to right or left her head,

* His

† baits

But go straight on. She has tasted elven bread.
And so, the story tells, she passed away
Out of the world: but if she dreams to-day
In fairy land, or if she wakes in Hell,*
(The chance being one in ten) it doesn't† tell.

     * In fairy *woods* or *dies and* wakes in Hell,

       † I cannot

NOTES

Lewis's own chronological account of the creation of *Dymer*, *Lewis Papers*, Vol. IX, pp. 129–30.

The prose version of Dymer.—1916

The 'Redemption of Ask'.—(In two parts, Lucrece metre.)—October and November 1918

The 'Red Maid' (ballad).—1920

Dymer begun.—April 2nd, 1922

Canto I finished.—May 11th, 1922

Canto II finished.—June 1st, 1922

Canto III (A-version) abandoned.—June 22nd, 1922

Canto III (B) finished.—June 29th, 1922

'Lyrical Epilogue' for Dymer attempted.—July 8th, 1922

Canto IV finished.—October 8th, 1922

Canto V finished.—March 25th, 1923

Canto V recopied and corrected.—June 27th, 1923

'Kirkian' stanzas done for Canto VI.—June 28th, 1923

'Kirkian' episode abandoned.—June 29th, 1923

Cantos VI and VII (A-version) finished.—September 8th, 1923. (Village shop and boat.)

Cantos VI and VII condemned by Harwood.—October 21st, 1923

Canto VI (B) finished.—October (?) 1923. (Old Welkin and boat.)

Canto III (C) finished.—January 22nd, 1924. (The cow version.)

Canto VI (C) finished.—March 25th, 1924

Canto IX finished.—March 25th, 1924

Canto VII (B) begun.—April 6th, 1924

Fresh start on Canto VII (B).—April 10th, 1924

Canto VII (B) finished.—(Complete text now in existence. Condemned.)—April 28th, 1924

Canto VI (D) started.—April or May 1924

Canto VI (D) finished.—Before May 23rd, 1924

Canto VII (C) and VIII.—Long Vacation 1925 (?)

Accepted by Dent's.—April 1st, 1926

Note 2

Lewis's introductory note to his alliterative poem, *The Nameless Isle*.

Every verse contains two half-verses. Each half-verse contains two beats or accents: and two dips which may consist of any number of unaccented syllables. The dips and beats may be arranged:

    a. In falling rhythm (*—u—u*) (*—uu—uu*) (*—u—uu*), etc.

> e.g. Eárly at évening
>
> Máster máriner

    b. In rising rhythm (*u—u—*) (*uu—uu—*) (*u—uu—*), etc.

> e.g. of the mén was Í
>
> While fást and fáir

    c. In clashing rhythm (*uu— —uu*) (*u— —u*), etc.

> e.g. In a spríng seáson
>
> Over our shíp scúdding

    d. As beat-dip-beat, without a second dip, if the single dip contains a syllable so strong that it nearly equals a beat (⸫ *—u—*) (⸫ ⸍*uu—*).

> e.g. Eíghteén in áll
>
> wítch-heárted quéen

The reader should read all with its natural accent and carefully avoid the artificial accents of syllabic verse

> e.g. Of the *séa*'s rísing

not, as it would be in the heroic line

> Óf the sea's rísing múch he spoke in vain.

There may be either two or three alliterations in the verse, of which only one can fall in the second half-verse.

All vowels alliterate together.

Note 3

Letters from John Masefield to C. S. Lewis about *The Queen of Drum*. Masefield's address is given as Pinbury, Cirencester on all the letters.

Dear Mr Lewis,

    Many thanks for the typescript safely received this morning. I will read it at once.

    With all good wishes,

> Yours sincerely,
>
> John Masefield

Dear Mr Lewis,

    I could not write to you during the week-end about *The Queen of Drum*. I wanted to go through it a second time; now I feel, that I must go through it again.

    Please let me say now, that I have greatly enjoyed it, and feel an extraordinary beauty in the main theme—the escape of the Queen into Fairyland.

    At present, I cannot help feeling, that the design is encumbered. I think that I see your intention, but, as a showman, I find that the second canto, the long talk with the Archbishop and the martydom of the Archbishop, are sagas in themselves, and diminish the poignancy of your main theme. Whenever your Queen appears, there is imagination, beauty and tension.

I wish to read the poem again during today; after that, I will write again; but I want you to have my first impressions for what they are worth, at once.

In any case, let me thank you for a great enjoyment. One might say of your Queen what Yeats' poet says:

'She need but lift a pearl pale hand
And all men's hearts must burn and beat.'

Yours sincerely,
John Masefield

Dear Mr Lewis,

I must apologise for having kept your *Queen of Drum* rather a long time. I wanted to read it again. I have much enjoyed it, but do feel, that the second canto is wrong, and that the Archbishop makes a saga by himself.

Then, on Page 55, the Crescent moon would not have risen; it would have become visible. It would have been in the sky at sunset, and the sky's darkening would have let it appear.

Please forgive this little note.

Let me thank you once more for the great pleasure that your poem has given me.

Yours sincerely,
John Masefield

Dear Mr Lewis,

So many thanks for your letter.

I was not troubled about the light later on in the canto. That passed as the light that never was on sea or land.

I am sorry that I left it in any doubt. Of course, we want the *Queen of Drum* in the Diversions. It is a very fine thing, and very beautiful; but the great difficulty is one of length. I feel that your story, as it stands, is too long, and that certain incidents in it detach fairly readily from your main theme. If you keep your Chancellor, will you consider getting rid of the Archbishop?

Of course, in matters of poetry,

'All is, if you have grace to use it so.'

You may have the power of making the Archbishop extraordinarily affecting.

I always feel that modern audiences begin to squirm and shuffle after about forty minutes. Do you think that you could bring the story into this compass?

I am grateful to you for your kind words about my work.

It would be a great pleasure to us both, if you would come over sometime to lunch or tea. This place is only about eighty minutes from Oxford. Will you think of this as a possibility on some Sunday?

Yours sincerely,
John Masefield